D1606002

Palgrave Studies in Race, Ethnicity, Indigeneity and Criminal Justice

Series Editors
Chris Cunneen
University of Technology Sydney
Sydney, NSW, Australia

Katheryn Russell-Brown
University of Florida
Gainesville, FL, USA

Shaun L. Gabbidon
Penn State Harrisburg
Middletown, PA, USA

Steve Garner
School of Social Sciences
Birmingham City University
Birmingham, UK

This pioneering series brings much-needed attention to minority, excluded, and marginalised perspectives in criminology, centred on the topic of 'race' and the racialization of crime and criminal justice systems. It draws on a range of theoretical approaches including critical race theory, critical criminology, postcolonial theory, intersectional approaches and Indigenous theory. The series seeks to challenge and broaden the current discourse, debates and discussions within contemporary criminology as a whole, including drawing on the voices of Indigenous people and those from the Global South which are often silenced in favour of dominant white discourses in Criminology.

More information about this series at
http://www.palgrave.com/gp/series/15777

Ivan Y. Sun · Yuning Wu

Race, Immigration, and Social Control

Immigrants' Views on the Police

palgrave
macmillan

Ivan Y. Sun
University of Delaware
Newark, DE, USA

Yuning Wu
Wayne State University
Detroit, MI, USA

Palgrave Studies in Race, Ethnicity, Indigeneity and Criminal Justice
ISBN 978-1-349-95806-1   ISBN 978-1-349-95807-8   (eBook)
https://doi.org/10.1057/978-1-349-95807-8

Library of Congress Control Number: 2018938313

Cover credit: macroworld/Getty Images

Printed on acid-free paper

This Palgrave Macmillan imprint is published by the registered company Macmillan Publishers Ltd. part of Springer Nature
The registered company address is: The Campus, 4 Crinan Street, London, N1 9XW, United Kingdom

Foreword

This timely book contributes to the national discussion of immigration policy, particularly its effects on law enforcement and the police. It examines critical issues in the policing of immigrants, such as do immigrants pose a threat to public safety, are there differences in criminality among immigrant groups, what issues do police face in dealing with immigrants, what are the attitudes of immigrants to the police, are these affected by whether immigrants are legal or illegal, and can police enforce immigration laws and at the same time protect immigrants from discrimination, exploitation, and violence.

It is tempting to summarize Sun's and Wu's answers, but that would be unfair. They deserve full credit for having the courage to raise these controversial issues and examining them with compelling scholarship and insight. So instead, I shall highlight elements in their presentation.

The heart of their analysis is an examination of the experience and attitudes of three distinct immigrant groups—Latinos, Chinese, and Arabs. Although the authors carefully discuss the histories of each group in the United States, they concentrate on new immigrants largely from the 1990s and early years of the twenty-first century. Similarly, their research draws mostly on scholarly studies and surveys from these same years.

For each migrant group, Sun and Wu examine differences in law enforcement policies. They also compare attitudes of each group toward the police, instructively analyzing reasons for these differences, such as predispositions from experiences in their home countries as well as in the United States. They pay particular attention to whether race, in addition to ethnicity, plays a role in immigrant–police relations.

The book discusses the dilemma confronting police in dealing with new immigrants. Can police contribute to enforcing rules against illegal immigration while at the same time protecting immigrants from criminality and sometimes violent discrimination? In short, can police enforce laws as well as protect people? The book concludes with suggestions about how this might be done, recognizing the tension between these objectives.

The writing of the book is sensibly informed by research, noting gaps in existing studies. It is also well organized and easy to read, with a delightful absence of jargon. Altogether Sun and Wu have corrected misinformation about the immigrant experience as well as avoiding overgeneralizations about it among immigrant communities.

David H. Bayley
Distinguished Professor Emeritus
School of Criminal Justice
University at Albany
Albany, USA

Acknowledgements

This book reflects and abridges some of our collective research efforts on public opinions on legal authorities over the past decade. We started with a 2006 piece on *Journal of Criminal Justice* assessing the impact of race, gender, and recent experience on people's perceptions of the courts. Over the years, the scope and depth of our studies, with the police as the focal concern, have substantially extended. We published a number of articles examining the effects of various individual, situational, and structural factors on people's evaluations of the police, domestically and internationally. The overarching goal of our research nonetheless remains unchanged—concerning equality and justice in the protection and application of the law.

As immigrants ourselves, we are blessed to have arrived and settled in this great country. As criminologists, we feel obligated and passionate about telling stories of immigrants' experience and subjectivity, including their relationship with regulatory authorities. Crimes committed by undocumented immigrants have rhetorically been used by candidates of political campaigns to advocate a tighter control of these populations, and the Trump administration has launched highly restrictive immigration policies and measures that could have a profound impact on many sectors of society, including law enforcement and immigrant communities. All these new developments further the need to have a systematic and accurate understanding of how the police work in immigrant communities and how the police are perceived by minority immigrant groups.

Considering both home country backgrounds and host country experiences, it is not a surprise to find immigrants' views of the police a highly complex phenomenon shaped by a combination of universal and specific factors. Issues of race, ethnicity, and culture intertwine to structure immigrants' lives, define their treatment by law enforcement, and mold their collective sentiments. When growing evidences suggest that the vast majority of immigrants are not more crime-prone than native-born Americans, our decade-long research findings indicate that they do not display stronger antiauthority sentiments than nonimmigrants either, despite being frequently targeted by law enforcement under the concerns of terrorism and national security.

A book is inevitably a collective product of many individuals. We are indebted to Professor Nicholas Lovrich, who kindly read through the entire manuscript and offered many valuable suggestions to our writing. A special thanks to Professor David Bayley, who found time out of his busy retirement life to write the preface for this book. Two University of Delaware doctoral students, Lindy Liu and Wenjin Wang, provided excellent assistance in checking references and making index of the book. Our appreciation also goes to Josie Taylor and Steph Carey of Palgrave Macmillan for their assistance and guidance in the process of producing this book. Last and most importantly, the unconditional support from our family members, particularly our spouse Mei and Leilei, makes this book possible. We hope that our collaboration on the subject matter continues and we are able to furnish you with a sequel a decade later.

Newark, DE, USA   Ivan Y. Sun
Detroit, MI, USA   Yuning Wu

Contents

List of Tables

1

Introduction

Immigrants[1] and immigration issues occupied a center stage position during the 2016 presidential election campaign. The Republican candidate Donald Trump on many occasions during the campaign made derogatory comments about Mexican immigrants, calling them criminals, rapists and drug smugglers, and repeatedly promised to build a wall along the United States (U.S.)–Mexico border to keep them away. Immediately after taking office in January 2017, President Trump signed a series of executive orders designed to overhaul the country's immigration system in the direction of more difficult entry for illegal and legal immigrants alike. In March and September, President Trump twice issued Executive Orders featuring travel bans, ranging from suspended immigrant and non-immigrant travel to permitting travel for non-immigrants with additional scrutiny, on people from eight mainly Muslim countries. In addition, reflecting the newly elected President's public policy priorities, in April 2017 the U.S. Department of Justice

---

[1]Immigrants in this book can refer to foreign-born individuals (first-generation), US-born individuals who have at least one foreign-born parent (second-generation), or both depending on context. Thus, immigrants and Americans are sometimes used interchangeably.

© The Author(s) 2018
I. Y. Sun and Y. Wu, *Race, Immigration, and Social Control*,
Palgrave Studies in Race, Ethnicity, Indigeneity and Criminal Justice,
https://doi.org/10.1057/978-1-349-95807-8_1

(DOJ) warned major sanctuary cities,[2] such as San Francisco, New York, Chicago, Los Angeles, and Philadelphia, that their federal grant funds would be in jeopardy if they did not comply fully with federal immigrant law. In October, DOJ delivered a "last chance" notice to sanctuary cities urging them to reconsider their policies on immigration before the federal government took action against them. In September 2017, the Trump administration announced its intention to end the *Deferred Action for Childhood Arrivals* (DACA) program, a 2012 initiative taken by President Obama by Executive Order that grants temporary protection from deportation to an estimated 800,000 individuals who arrived in the U.S. illegally as children.

The most recent wave of **anti-immigration** activism in the U.S. has become a centrepiece of the new Administration. Albeit still early in his presidency, Donald Trump has deliberately engineered a major crackdown on immigration at a national level that has not been witnessed for many decades. Although this is not the first time in American history that immigrants have been aggressively and discriminatorily targeted, the current Administration's anti-immigration rhetoric and arbitrary approach remain highly controversial and undoubtedly cast a profoundly dark shadow on many aspects of social life in much of American society. This is particularly the case within communities where immigrants are welcomed as valued members of their communities and within immigrant communities and families.

Historically, the U.S. has been a nation of immigrants. The U.S. foreign-born population (i.e., those who were not U.S. citizens at birth) has nearly **tripled** over the past five decades, increasing from 4.7% in 1970 to 12.9% in 2010. The largest shares of immigrants during the past decade are from Latin American and Asian countries, contrasting with the foreign-born from mostly European countries who immigrated to the U.S. in the 1960s and earlier. The topic of immigration has been a controversial issue in political and public discourse for a very long time, with some heated debates surrounding the crime, public safety

---

[2]Sanctuary cities refer to jurisdictions that limit local law enforcement officials' cooperation with the federal government in enforcing immigration law.

and policing dimensions of the issue. Scholars have long scrutinized the relationship between the police and minority immigrant groups in the U.S., often documenting tensions, discrimination, and differential treatment at the hands of local police. Indeed, the history of American policing is replete with examples of serious and sustained conflict between local police and various minority immigrant groups.

The primary purpose of this book is to discuss a range of issues surrounding race, ethnicity, and immigrant status in U.S. policing, with a special focus on immigrant groups' perceptions of the police and factors that shape their attitudes toward law enforcement. We utilize research approaches such as historical, etiological, and comparative analyses, and we analyze both original and secondary data. Our goal is to not only systematically introduce relevant evidence and theoretical models related to immigrants' assessments of the police, but to also shed light on potential challenges and difficulties that legal authorities are likely to face during an era of increasingly tightened control over immigrant populations in the country.

The Interplay of Race/Ethnicity, Immigration and Policing

While crime and justice researchers have explored the past and current potential links between immigration and crime, immigrants' perceptions of their local police have largely been ignored. This is the case even though immigrants' views of the police most likely have important implications for policing, in particular with respect to police-community relations. Moreover, issues arising from the intersection of immigration, race/ethnicity and policing are not unique to the U.S. This combination of factors has produced large-scale unrest in French, Dutch and English cities and townships alike in recent decades. Positive police images encourage voluntary support and promote cooperation from immigrants, which is critical for controlling crime and maintaining order in today's increasingly multi-ethnic, multi-cultural and globally oriented society. Police-community relations in ethnically diverse population centers may be strained by a host of immigrant-specific issues, including matters of language incompatibilities and cultural barriers, adverse country of origin experiences with corrupt and/or incompetent police, and immigration status-related legal issues. Recent federal agency requests for local police departments to enforce federal immigration law often further complicate relations between local police and the publics they serve. Given these concerns, the research base on citizens' views on the police needs to be broadened and deepened to include various distinct immigrant groups and immigrant-specific issues.

The investigation of immigrants' perceptions of the police has both theoretical and practical significance. Theoretically, understanding immigrants' attitudes toward the police fills a gap in the literature on public evaluations of the police, a literature which has seldom taken into serious account the interplay of race/ethnicity and immigrant status in shaping such attitudes. Specifically, knowledge of this kind advances the theoretical development of public opinion on the police by shedding light on whether various factors found in previous research to be predictive of White and Black Americans' perceptions of the police can be applied to racial majority and minority immigrants. Put into practical terms, information about immigrants' attitudes toward the police provides valuable baseline evidence, allowing law enforcement agencies to implement suitable policies and practices for policing immigrant communities.

Research relying heavily upon the dichotomous White–Black division or the White-Other-Black racial gradient misses the complex dynamics of contemporary police-community relations and grossly oversimplifies the diversity present across minority groups. Non-Black minority groups, many immigrant groups included, have not been incorporated into current analysis to a sufficient degree. Without addressing these groups' unique characteristics and experiences, a theoretical framework that aims to explain public perceptions of the police cannot be complete. In this book, we take the initiative to chart the experience and perceptions of Hispanic, Chinese and Arab immigrants, documenting not only the variations, but also the commonalities across groups. Effectively integrating past research, we propose an integrated conceptual model that includes both general factors that tend to influence public evaluations of the police for all racial/ethnic groups as well as immigrant-specific factors that are likely to shape immigrants' perceptions only.

This conceptual model incorporates a variety of existent theories and proposes new ones that intend to uncover the sociological structure, culture, and process that may contribute to group differential views on the police. It is hoped that this model can to a certain extent relieve the current sore limitation of lacking guiding theoretical frameworks in data analysis in studies on immigrant perceptions of the police. Altogether, it is hoped that this book may engender more interest in theoretically guided empirical research on immigrant minority perceptions of the police. This is the main rationale behind the writing of this book.

A Focus on Three Immigrant Groups

The book strategically chooses to elaborate on the perceptions of three rapidly growing yet understudied ethnic groups—namely, Hispanic/ Latino, Chinese, and Arab Americans. Discussion of their perceptions of and experience with the police revolves around several central themes, those being *theoretical frameworks*, *historical developments*, *contemporary perceptions*, and *emerging challenges*.

These specific immigrant groups are selected at this particular time for several compelling reasons. Latinos represent the largest minority group in the U.S., and—along with Asian Americans—have been the fastest growing group in this country. Similarly, for Arab Americans, between 2000 and 2010 there was an approximate 47% increase in the population size of this group. In addition, all these groups have diverse groups within their communities that reject a simplistic, overgeneralized view on their perceptions of the police. For example, the varying racial identities (i.e., White, Black, and non-White and non-Black) among Hispanics and Arabs and the substantial disparities in socioeconomic status and immigration backgrounds among Chinese immigrants make their assessments of the police complicated, requiring a more nuanced understanding of public perceptions of police in

America. Finally, the terrorist attacks of September 11, 2001 (hereafter referred to as "9/11") have made almost all groups of immigrants living in the U.S., especially people who have an Arab ethnic, cultural and linguistic heritage, more visible groups for law enforcement attention. The current focus on Hispanic, Chinese and Arab immigrants facilitates our identification and summary of some common themes across major immigrant populations, and serves as a springboard for launching future research on other immigrant groups who may be less visible and large in population in the nation.

The Organization of the Book

This book consists of eight chapters, with three to four sections present in each chapter. Chapter 2 focuses on three major themes surrounding the role of race and ethnicity in U.S. policing, including relevant theoretical explanations for minorities' attitudes toward the police, official statistics and empirical evidence related to racial/ethnic differences in arrests, use of deadly force, and traffic stops, and the race and ethnicity influence on public evaluations of the police. Chapter 3 discusses the ideologies, beliefs and theories that underline social control strategies toward immigrants developed in the U.S., explains how a variety of immigrant groups were treated and policed historically, clarifies the complex connection obtaining between immigrant groups and their records of criminal offending, and delineates challenges faced by the police in establishing and maintaining public order and protecting an increasingly diverse immigrant population before and after the 9/11 terrorist attacks.

In Chapters 4–6 we focus on three immigrant groups: Latinos, Chinese, and Arabs. In these chapters, we first describe the historical and contemporary backgrounds of these immigrant populations in the U.S., followed by discussions on social control exercised by legal authorities and the relationships between the police and these immigrant groups. We then discuss the general patterns of immigrants' evaluations of the police and factors that shape their attitudes toward the police.

Chapter 7 is devoted to a thorough review of the empirical evidence reported in systematic research involving the comparison of attitudes toward the police across two or more minority groups in the U.S. This chapter importantly features the introduction of a new conceptual framework that can help explain immigrant minority attitudes toward police. The last chapter (Chapter 8) concludes with reflections on our principal findings in this book and suggestions on how to improve police-immigrant community relations in the U.S.

2

Race/Ethnicity as the Defining Characteristic of Policing in the U.S.

Race/ethnicity is arguably one of the most influential characteristics of social affairs in the U.S. Various forms of racism and racial inequality, such as residential and school segregation, discrimination in employment and access to public services, and profiling in law enforcement and disproportionate minority contact in the criminal justice system, have placed tremendous burdens on racial and ethnic minorities since the early days of American history. The last several decades have witnessed some noteworthy advancement in the social, political, economic, and educational rights and social status of people of color and noticeable changes in the operation of the criminal justice system clearly resulting from the civil rights movement. Some researchers argue that the importance of racial background is diminishing in the daily lives of Americans (Wilson, 1987), including in predicting citizen evaluations of the police (Jesilow, Meyer, & Namazzi, 1995). Others, however, contend that racial inequality remains ordinary rather than aberrational (Delgado & Stefancic, 2001). Racial minorities, especially in urban high crime areas, continue to have strained relationship with the police (Walker, Spohn, & DeLone, 2003), and the persisting social distance between Whites and Blacks continues to allow the nation to be

© The Author(s) 2018
I. Y. Sun and Y. Wu, *Race, Immigration, and Social Control,*
Palgrave Studies in Race, Ethnicity, Indigeneity and Criminal Justice,
https://doi.org/10.1057/978-1-349-95807-8_2

characterized as containing two societies—one Black, one White, separate and unequal (Hacker, 1992).

The large influx of immigrants after the World War II has made the U.S. population increasingly diverse with respect to cultural heritage and racial/ethnic composition. It is predicted by demographers that America will become a nation of minorities by 2050, with Whites being a numerical "minority" (Chideya, 2006). This is not surprising given that recent immigrants are most likely to come from Latin America, the Caribbean, and Asia, contrasting with the nation's foreign-born individuals hailing from mostly European countries in the past. The rapid transformation of the racial composition of the U.S. has challenged the traditional Black–White framework of studying race and ethnicity, which fails to account for the diverse experiences *between* Whites and non-Black minorities and *within* and *among* the nation's various minority groups.

Race/ethnicity defines relationships, resources, and identities (Higginbotham & Anderson, 2012) as well as affects the relative efficacy of social control strategies in the country. Before World War II, social control of racial and ethnic minorities, particularly African Americans, was carried out through both informal mechanisms (e.g., slave patrol) and written and unwritten rules (e.g., the Jim Crow laws and practices). After the War, such control was exercised almost exclusively by state apparatus (Marable, 1983), with the police playing a central role in formal social control over racial/ethnic minorities. The post-civil rights era of social control is still plagued by widespread reports of police brutality and misconduct, disparities and bias in arrest and incarceration rates, and lower levels of minority trust and confidence in the police. Recent tragic events in Ferguson, New York City, and Baltimore elucidate the interconnectedness of these phenomena and their profound impact on public perceptions of racial injustice and bias policing in the country.

In this chapter, we discuss three major themes surrounding the role of race and ethnicity in the U.S. policing. First, we revisit relevant theoretical explanations for minorities' attitudes toward the police. Second, we report official statistics and provide empirical evidence related to racial/ethnic differences in three common forms of police control actions—arrests, use of deadly force, and traffic stops. Finally, we discuss how race and ethnicity influence public evaluations of the police.

Theoretical Reappraisal

Two theoretical frameworks have been articulated to explain why White and minority Americans tend to perceive of the police differently. Originating from social psychology (Berger, Zelditch, & Anderson, 1972; Deutsch & Krauss, 1965; Runciman, 1966), the *sense-of-injustice* model posits that public assessments of criminal justice agencies are profoundly influenced by the feeling of being treated unjustly by the gatekeepers of "the system," in this case the police officers (Wu, Sun, & Triplett, 2009). Relating this argument to race, minorities—most especially African Americans—tend to display less positive attitudes toward the police because they are more likely than White Americans to have a sense of unequal treatment by the criminal justice system in general and the police in particular. Such a higher level of sense-of-injustice among Blacks can be attributed chiefly to their over-representation as both offenders and victims in the U.S.

The core arguments of the sense-of-injustice model are parallel to the propositions of comparative conflict theory, which proposes that minorities perceive more injustice than any other racial category, and minorities who have contacts with the criminal justice system are differentially impacted and their perceptions change from these experiences (Hagan, Shedd, & Payne, 2005). Minority citizens frame their perceptions of injustice from a historical and social perspective, which tend to be formed during their youth. This theory also proposes that Hispanics should perceive less injustice than African Americans, because not only do Hispanics have a less intensive history of discriminatory treatment within the U.S., but also because Whites and their agents of social control tend to view Hispanics as less threatening than African Americans due to their lighter skin tone (Buckler & Unnever, 2008; Buckler, Unnever, & Cullen, 2008; Hagan et al., 2005).

The central propositions of the sense-of-injustice model also echo findings from studies on procedural justice which suggest that people's perceptions of local legal authorities, including the police, are primarily impacted by whether they perceive such agencies as fair and equitable in both the procedures for making decisions and the outcomes of their decisions (Tyler, 1990). Low perceptions of police legitimacy may lead to low legal compliance and cooperation with the police, poor police-community relations, and even high crime rates (Anderson, 1999; LaFree, 1998; Tyler, 1990, 2003).

A second model that has been employed to explicate the persisting minority-White differences in attitudes toward the police is the *group-position perspective*. Originating from Blumer's (1958) group-position theory of racial prejudice, and extended by Weitzer and Tuch's (2005, 2006) research on pubic evaluations of the police, this model maintains that individual orientations toward social institutions spring primarily from a sense of group position that involves the core elements of "group identity, out-group stereotyping, preferred group status, and perceived threat" (Bobo & Hutchings, 1996, p. 955). Specifically, members of the dominant group (i.e., the in-group) tend to share a sense of superiority, view members of the subordinate group (i.e., the out-group) as intrinsically different and alien, display a claim over certain rights, social statuses, privileges and resources, and perceive out-group members as significant competitors for such resources and prerogatives (Bobo & Tuan, 2006). This perspective resembles Blalock's (1967) racial threat theory which posits that the increased presence and visibility of minority groups are viewed by Whites as economic and political threats.

Extending these arguments to racial attitudes toward the police, Whites are more likely to hold positive opinions on the police because they regard this social institution as housing the protectors of their interests and social superiority. The stereotyping images of minorities commonly held by many Whites, particularly of African Americans (e.g., more violent and prone to crime), also promote their support for aggressive law enforcement actions against minorities and heavy patrolling of minority neighborhoods (Weitzer & Tuch, 2006). Racial prejudice associated with a sense of group position thus is likely one of the key factors differentiating minorities' and Whites' views on the police.

The common theme running through both the sense-of-injustice and group-position model is that minorities are more likely than Whites to be treated unjustly and unfairly by the criminal justice system, including by the police, which consequently influences minorities' attitudes toward the police. Before presenting empirical evidence on racial differences in attitudes toward the police, the primary source of such distinctions in attitudes possibly resulting from police control actions is discussed.

Disparity or Bias in Police Control

As the primary agents of social control, the police are empowered with the authority to use coercion, including intruding into citizens' lives, restricting their liberty through detention or arrest, and using physical (even deadly) force in encounters with citizens if necessary. In this section, we focus our discussion on the connections between race/ethnicity and the three most visible and arguably influential types of police field interventions: arrests, use of deadly force, and traffic stops. These coercive approaches emphasize the exercise of authority or influence over the public to contain violence and control order. They include a range of activities widely recognized as necessary for accomplishing the primary operating goal for police officers (Sun, 2003; Sun & Payne, 2004). Below, we assess whether racial differences exist in these police control actions and, if so, whether they signal racial discrimination or differential treatment by the police, or simply constitute disparities that are not necessarily caused by any bias on the part of the police (Walker et al., 2003).

Arrest

Among coercive actions exercised by the police, arrest is the most frequently studied. In 2015, the U.S. state and local police agencies made more than 10 million arrests at a rate of 3200 per 100,000 inhabitants (Federal Bureau of Investigation 2015). A key concern of this most critical form of police coercion is that not only the U.S. has the highest crime rates and toughest criminal sanctions among industrialized countries (Bayley, 1994), but also police arrests are not proportionately distributed across racial/ethnic groups in American society.

Nationwide official statistics can illustrate this problem quite clearly. Table 2.1 displays the percentages of arrest for Whites, Blacks,

Table 2.1 Race of persons arrested, 1993–2016

Year	Total (%)				Violent crime[a] (%)				Property crime[b] (%)			
	White	Black	Native[c]	Asian[d]	White	Black	Native	Asian	White	Black	Native	Asian
1993	66.9	31.1	1.1	1.0	52.6	45.7	0.8	1.0	64.4	33.2	1.0	1.4
1994	66.6	31.3	1.1	1.0	53.4	44.7	0.8	1.1	64.4	33.1	1.0	1.4
1995	66.8	30.9	1.1	1.1	54.3	43.7	0.8	1.2	64.7	32.6	1.1	1.6
1996	66.9	30.7	1.3	1.2	54.6	43.2	0.9	1.3	64.7	32.4	1.2	1.7
1997	67.1	30.4	1.3	1.2	56.8	41.1	0.9	1.1	64.8	32.4	1.2	1.7
1998	68.0	29.7	1.2	1.1	57.7	40.2	1.0	1.1	65.3	31.9	1.2	1.6
1999	69.0	28.6	1.2	1.1	59.2	38.7	1.0	1.2	65.7	31.4	1.2	1.7
2000	69.7	27.9	1.2	1.2	59.9	37.8	1.0	1.3	66.2	31.0	1.2	1.6
2001	69.5	28.1	1.3	1.1	60.2	37.6	1.0	1.2	66.0	31.4	1.2	1.5
2002	70.7	27.9	1.3	1.1	59.7	38.0	1.1	1.2	67.7	29.6	1.2	1.5
2003	70.6	27.0	1.3	1.2	60.5	37.2	1.0	1.2	68.2	29.1	1.2	1.4
2004	70.5	27.1	1.3	1.1	60.5	37.2	1.1	1.1	69.0	28.5	1.2	1.3
2005	69.8	27.8	1.3	1.0	59.0	38.8	1.2	1.1	68.8	28.6	1.2	1.3
2006	69.7	28.0	1.3	1.1	58.5	39.3	1.1	1.1	68.2	29.4	1.1	1.2
2007	69.7	28.2	1.3	0.8	58.9	39.0	1.3	0.8	67.9	29.8	1.2	1.0
2008	69.3	28.3	1.3	1.1	58.3	39.4	1.1	1.1	67.4	30.1	1.2	1.3
2009	69.1	28.3	1.4	1.2	58.7	38.9	1.2	1.1	67.6	29.8	1.3	1.3
2010	69.4	28.0	1.4	1.2	59.3	38.1	1.3	1.2	68.4	28.9	1.3	1.3
2011	69.2	28.4	1.5	0.9	59.4	39.3	1.3	0.9	69.1	29.5	1.4	1.0
2012	69.3	28.1	1.4	1.2	58.7	38.5	1.3	1.4	68.0	29.3	1.4	1.3
2013	68.9	28.3	1.6	1.3	58.4	38.7	1.3	1.5	68.2	29.0	1.5	1.3
2014	69.4	27.8	1.6	1.2	59.4	37.7	1.4	1.6	68.8	28.4	1.5	1.3
2015	69.7	26.6	2.1	1.5	60.1	36.4	1.8	1.8	69.2	27.8	1.5	1.4
2016	69.6	26.9	2.0	1.5	59.0	37.5	1.8	1.7	68.7	28.1	1.7	1.5

Data sources FBI: UCR, retrieved online from http://ucr.fbi.gov
[a]Violent crimes include murder, non-negligent manslaughter, forcible rape, robbery, and aggravated assault
[b]Property crimes include burglary, larceny-theft, motor vehicle theft, and arson
[c]Refers to American Indians and Alaska Natives
[d]Refers to Asians and Pacific Islanders

American Indians and Alaska Natives, and Asians and Pacific Islanders over the period 1993–2016. The percentage for Whites showed a slightly upward trend, and the percentage for Blacks revealed a slightly downward tendency. Whites made up less than 70% of those arrested in recent years, which is nearly 10% lower than their share (79%) in the general population. Whites' underrepresentation is most evident in violent crimes, which was around 60% in recent years. Among racial minorities of Black, Asian, and Native Americans, compared to their percentages in the general population (12.8%, 4.6%, and 1%, respectively), Blacks were overrepresented particularly for violent crime arrests, whereas Asian Americans were underrepresented, with Native Americans having a rate higher than their population. The likelihood of African Americans to be arrested for violent and property crimes was over 3 and 2.5 times, separately, greater than their proportion in the U.S. population. Over a 30-year period from 1980 to 2009, the Black–White contrast is most discernible in murder and robbery, with the Black arrest rates averaging 7 and 10 times the White rates, respectively (Snyder, 2011). Although the country's total crime rate has shown a downward trend since the early 1990s, Blacks have been—and continue to be—subject to a much higher rate of arrest than Whites and other racial minorities for nearly all categories of crime.

The racial difference in the percentage of those arrested for Whites and Blacks is even striking for those who were under 18 years old. As shown in Table 2.2, African-American youth constituted more than half of the violent crime arrests and one-third of the property crime arrests in the country since 2006. That is, among juvenile arrests, one in every two violent crime arrests and one in every three property crime arrests involved African-American youth. Furthermore, while the national statistics for Blacks arrested reveal a downward trend, the percentages for Black juveniles arrested for both violent and property crimes were on the rise, increasing from 47.2% in 1996 to 52.0% for violent crime and from 26.4% in 1996 to 38.2% for property crime in 2016. A recent study found that young Black males between 18 and 23 were also more likely to experience arrests than their White male counterparts (Brame, Bushway, Paternoster, & Turner, 2014). Black juveniles and young men are much more vulnerable to police arrests than their White counterparts.

Table 2.2 Race of persons arrested under 18 years of age, 1996–2016

Year	Total (%)				Violent crime[a] (%)				Property crime[b] (%)			
	White	Black	Native[c]	Asian[d]	White	Black	Native	Asian	White	Black	Native	Asian
1996	69.7	27.3	1.2	1.3	50.3	47.2	0.8	1.7	69.9	26.4	1.4	2.3
1997	70.6	26.5	1.3	1.7	53.4	44.2	0.8	1.5	69.9	26.6	1.4	2.1
1998	71.3	26.0	1.1	1.6	55.3	42.3	0.9	1.5	70.1	26.6	1.3	2.0
1999	71.9	25.1	1.3	1.7	56.8	40.6	1.0	1.6	69.3	27.1	1.4	2.2
2000	72.1	25.1	1.2	1.7	55.4	42.1	0.9	1.6	69.4	27.3	1.3	2.0
2001	70.9	26.4	1.2	1.5	55.2	42.5	0.9	1.4	68.5	28.4	1.3	1.8
2002	71.5	25.7	1.3	1.6	54.7	42.8	1.0	1.4	69.6	27.2	1.3	1.9
2003	70.6	26.6	1.3	1.6	52.7	45.0	0.9	1.4	69.0	27.7	1.4	1.9
2004	69.3	28.1	1.2	1.4	51.8	46.0	0.9	1.3	68.5	28.4	1.4	1.8
2005	67.5	29.9	1.3	1.3	48.2	49.8	0.9	1.1	67.2	29.8	1.3	1.6
2006	67.1	30.3	1.1	1.4	47.0	51.0	1.1	1.1	66.3	30.9	1.1	1.7
2007	67.7	30.8	1.2	1.0	47.5	50.7	0.9	0.9	65.7	31.8	1.2	1.3
2008	66.4	30.9	1.2	1.5	46.4	51.6	0.7	1.1	64.7	32.6	1.1	1.6
2009	65.9	31.3	1.2	1.6	46.4	51.6	0.8	1.2	63.9	33.2	1.2	1.7
2010	66.3	31.1	1.2	1.4	47.5	50.5	0.9	1.1	64.0	33.0	1.2	1.8
2011	65.7	32.0	1.3	1.0	47.0	51.4	0.9	0.7	62.4	35.0	1.3	1.3
2012	65.2	32.2	1.3	1.2	46.6	51.5	0.8	1.0	61.6	35.5	1.3	1.7
2013	63.0	34.4	1.5	1.2	44.8	53.3	0.9	1.0	59.7	37.2	1.5	1.6
2014	63.0	34.5	1.4	1.2	45.6	52.4	0.9	1.1	59.6	37.6	1.4	1.4
2015	62.9	33.9	1.7	1.5	46.8	50.8	1.1	1.3	59.1	37.7	1.5	1.8
2016	62.1	34.7	1.7	1.5	45.5	52.0	1.2	1.5	58.4	38.2	1.7	1.7

Data sources FBI: UCR, retrieved online from http://ucr.fbi.gov
[a]Violent crimes include murder, non-negligent manslaughter, forcible rape, robbery, and aggravated assault
[b]Property crimes include burglary, larceny-theft, motor vehicle theft, and arson
[c]Refers to American Indians and Alaska Natives
[d]Refers to Asians and Pacific Islanders

Controversy remains regarding the factors underlying the dramatic overrepresentation of minorities in arrests. A substantial number of studies have been conducted to examine the issue in detail. Some studies have found that officers were more likely to arrest or use improper force against African-American suspects when controlling for other variables, such as offense seriousness and suspect demeanor (e.g., Brown & Frank, 2006; Smith & Visher, 1981; Spano, 2003; Sun, Payne, & Wu, 2008; Withrow, 2004; Worden, 1996, whereas other researchers 1995). The most convincing evidence supporting a linkage between suspect race and police arrests came from a recent meta-analysis of 40 research reports, which found that *the effect size of race varied between 1.32 and 1.52; that is, compared to the average probability of a White being arrested (.20), the average probability for a non-White was .26* (Kochel, Wilson, & Mastrofski, 2011).

With respect to officer race, some researchers have reported that White, African American, and Hispanic officers acted similarly (e.g., Smith & Klein, 1984; Worden, 1989), but others have reported a connection between officer race and arrest and coercive behavior (Brooks, 2001; Brown & Frank, 2006; Fyfe, 1988; Geller & Scott, 1992; Sun & Payne, 2004). In addition, the relationship between the racial composition of police departments and arrest rates for Blacks versus Whites has also been examined. Some evidence reported in the research literature has indicated that no significant association obtained (Slovak, 1986), but some researchers have found that increases in White officers were associated with increases in non-White arrests, and increases in non-White officers were associated with increases in White arrests (Donohue & Levitt, 2001). The racial composition of the police force has also been found to moderate the connection between offender race and the probability of arrest for simple assaults (Eitle, Stolzenberg, & D'Alessio, 2005).

While national aggregate statistics and research findings continue to reveal a higher arrest risk for Blacks, there is not enough evidence to conclude whether such racial differences in outcomes represent discrimination, or is there merely a disparity. Nonetheless, the relevance of race and the concern about the potential bias associated with police control stay alive and valid until racial equality is finally realized in the larger society.

Use of Deadly Force

Police use of deadly force represents a major source of police-minority confrontations in American policing (Walker & Katz, 2013). Before the 1980s, the use of deadly force was guided predominately by the so-called "fleeing felon" rule, which authorized officers to apply deadly force as a legitimate means of apprehending individuals who were fleeing from suspected felonies. Under this loosely-defined policy, police officers were entitled to greater discretion in distributing deadly force, which led to an uneven, adverse effect on socially disadvantaged and minority groups. Poor people and racial minorities, especially African Americans who lived in neighborhoods with low socio-economic status, high crime rates, and mediocre or poor police-community relations, were much more susceptible to deadly harm than those who lived in affluent and predominately White neighborhoods. Consequently, during the 1960s and 1970s, African Americans were 6–8 times more likely to be shot and killed by police officers than White Americans (Walker & Katz, 2013).

Goldkamp (1976) has proposed two competing perspectives to explain the incidence of racial disproportionality in police use of deadly force. The first view emphasized prejudice and discrimination embedded in police field practices. Officers were depicted to have "two trigger fingers" on their weapons, one for Whites and another for Blacks (Takagi, 1974). Patrol officers seemed to engage different mentalities when they drove around the streets of poor, minority neighborhoods as opposed to safer areas, where oftentimes issues of race and place are connected. The second perspective stressed that Blacks were disproportionately involved in criminal activities, particularly violent crimes, which increased their likelihood of being shot by the police. These perspectives imply that both predisposed attitudinal propensities and occupational socialization and cultures could affect officers' discretionary decisions in applying deadly force. Although research has yet to generate persuasive evidence to support the existence of either of Goldkamp's proposed perspectives, policy governing police use of deadly force has nonetheless evolved substantially since the 1970s.

In 1972, the New York City Police Department (NYPD) replaced the permissive fleeing felon standard with a more restrictive *defense-of-life rule*, a decisional guideline which permits the use of deadly force **only if the officer's life, the citizen's life, or another officer's life is in danger**. The adoption of the new policy drew national-wide attention because it reduced NYPD's firearms discharges substantially (by nearly a third) (Fyfe, 1979). In an important ruling from the nation's high court (*Tennessee v. Garner, 1985*), the U.S. Supreme Court ruled that the fleeing felon doctrine was unconstitutional because it violated the Fourth Amendment's guarantees against unreasonable seizure. This momentous decision officially ended the use of the fleeing felon rule.

Previous studies have consistently shown that police use of force in general, and use of deadly force in particular, are rather rare events. For example, NYPD officers reported the application of a firearm in only 5 incidents among a total of 1762 occasions in which physical force was employed to subdue a subject (New York State Commission of Criminal Justice, 1987). In other words, only 4% of use of physical force cases involved deadly force. In New Jersey, police agencies in the entire state responded to 8.5 million calls in 1991 and officers fired their weapons on only 167 occasions, resulting in a rate of lower than 0.02% (Sullivan, 1992).

Police statistics indicated that the more restrictive defense-of-life policy has resulted in not only fewer police killings of citizens, but also lower racial disparity in use of force incidents (Tennenbaum, 1994). For instance, in Memphis, Tennessee, police fatally shot a total of 34 suspected fleeing felons (8 Whites and 26 Blacks) between 1970 and 1974, the five-year period before the *Garner* case, and the number of fatal shootings reduced to 19 (7 Whites and 12 Blacks) between 1985 and 1989. It appears that the likelihood-of-being-killed gap between Whites and Blacks has narrowed to a considerably extent, but nevertheless persists.

The reason of why Blacks are more likely to be subject to police deadly force remains unsettled, with some scholars suggesting the essential role of individual officer differences (Fyfe, 1982; Meyer, 1980) whereas others contending the primacy of situational considerations (Matulia, 1985; White, 2002). It is plausible that officers' decisions to use deadly force on minorities could be influenced by a combination of multiple factors. Patrol officers may anticipate a greater risk of violent confrontations when working in lower-class minority neighborhoods and correspondingly employ a higher level of coercion. Non-cooperative and hostile attitudes and behavior displayed by young, minority persons could be perceived by officers as greater challenges and threats to their authority and thus are exposed to higher levels of control. It is also likely that the use of deadly force to tame members of socially disadvantaged groups is deeply rooted in the police occupational culture that emphasizes authority and control over citizens, particularly racial and ethnic minorities (Chan, 1997; Crank, 2004; Skolnick, 1966). Variations in department size, policy, and level of professionalism may also affect officers' shooting behavior. Attempting to account for police use of deadly force, recent theoretical advancements and empirical investigations have greatly extended from situational and individual to social cultural, organizational, and structural and community explanations (Belur, 2010; Chan, 1997; Green & Ward, 2004; Willits & Nowacki, 2014; Worden, 1996). Such efforts should shed new light on the discrimination-disparity debate of the use of deadly force.

Traffic Stops

One of the most common traditional law enforcement activities is aggressive preventive patrol, which usually involves an enhanced level of patrol intervention through traffic stops and suspicious person stops. Research in this area has suggested that officers have exercised wide discretion in determining whether to initiate the contact, and in deciding what kind of intervention was appropriate as an result of the contact (for example, see Brown, 1988). Aggressive patrol, however, has long been recognized as having an adverse effect on public satisfaction with the police (President's Commission on Law Enforcement and Administration of Justice, 1967). Overly aggressive tactics are often not appreciated, especially by racial/ethnic minorities who are more likely to be stopped arbitrarily and perceive such police public safety interventions as unjustified harassment (Epp, Maynard-Moody, &

Haider-Markel, 2014). Therefore, unless police officers are uncommonly skillful in impartially enforcing traffic violations, in picking out truly suspicious people or drivers, and in persuading the public of the legitimacy and necessity of their aggressive practices, more citizen complaints would seem inevitable with an increase in aggressive preventive patrol interventions (Boydstun, 1975).

Traffic enforcement has become an even more powerful police tactic since the 1996 Supreme Court ruling, which held that officers may stop motorists for minor traffic violations even if their real motive is to look for evidence of serious crimes (*Whren et al. v. United States*, 1996). Officers frequently engage in stopping, questioning, and frisking suspicious people on their own initiative. To justify a field interrogation, the law requires that the police must be able to point to specific and articulable facts which, when considered together with the rational inferences drawn from those facts, create a reasonable suspicion of criminal conduct on the part of the suspect (*Terry v. Ohio*, 1968). Obviously, the definition of a 'specific' or 'articulable' fact is ambiguous and not so clear and assessable as that of a 'violation' prescribed in traffic laws, suggesting that officers' own interpretations of situations may justify the field stops.

The problems associated with the use of aggressive traffic enforcement surfaced in the 1990s when racial profiling involving police stopping drivers based merely on drivers' race and ethnicity drew widespread attention in the media. The phenomenon of DWB (driving while black or brown), DWA (driving while Asian) and DWF (driving while female) reported around the country casted serious doubt about the impartiality of police traffic enforcement. State police in New Jersey and Maryland were sued for their systematic engagement in racial profiling on interstate highways. New Jersey Attorney General Office found that nearly 60% of all traffic stops involved White drivers, but Blacks and Hispanics were targets of 53.1 and 24% of the searches, respectively, and of the 2871 arrests made, 61.7% were Blacks and 32.5% were Whites (New Jersey Attorney General Office, 1999). The American Civil Liberties Union (ACLU) found that while Blacks made up only 17.5% of drivers observed to be speeding on Maryland's highways, they represented 73% of all drivers who were stopped and searched by the police (American Civil Liberties Union, 1999).

To combat the virtual epidemic of racial profiling, many states have passed laws to make such practices illegal for public officials, including the police. Police agencies required officers to document drivers' race on their traffic report forms and instructed supervisors to randomly contact stopped drivers to verify their race/ethnicity. Many police departments also intensified their cultural diversity training for both the rank-and-file and agency managers. Although the public outcry over racial profiling seems to be receding in recent years, Black and Hispanics continue to experience greater police control during traffic stops during the 2000s.

Data from the Police–Public Contact Survey (PPCS), which was conducted by the Bureau of Justice Statistics, U.S. Department of Justice, indicated that nearly 17% of U.S. residents age 16 or older had a face-to-face contact with the police in 2008 (Eith & Durose, 2011). The most common reason for an encounter with the police (44.1%) was being a driver in a traffic stop. Whites were more likely than Blacks, Hispanics, and Asians to have contacts with the police, but the consequences resulting from traffic stops varied noticeably between White and minority drivers. Black drivers were about three times as likely as White drivers and about two times as likely as Hispanic drivers to be searched during a traffic stop. Similar patterns were found in previous PPCS data conducted in 2002 and 2005 (Durose, Schmitt, & Langan, 2005; Durose, Smith, & Langan, 2007).

Based on data collected from various jurisdictions, the vast majority of studies have confirmed that race/ethnicity matters in traffic stops, with Blacks being significantly more likely than Whites to be stopped (Roh & Robinson, 2009; Smith & Petrocelli, 2001; Warren, Tomaskovic-Devey, Smith, Zingraff, & Mason, 2006) and, equally importantly, be searched during traffic stops (Alpert, Dunham, & Smith, 2007; Engel & Calnon, 2004; Higgins, Jennings, Jordan, & Gabbidon, 2011; Schafer, Carter, Katz-Bannister, & Wells, 2006). While researchers were cautious about suggesting police traffic stops to be discriminative or prejudiced, police traffic stops and enforcement actions were certainly not evenly distributed across racial/ethnic groups. A combination effect of race and place was also identified, in which Blacks are especially subject to disproportionate surveillance and stopping by the police when driving through White areas (Meehan & Ponder, 2002). Research has also found that in highly segregated communities, police searches are more likely in stops of Black drivers than in those of White drivers, especially by White officers; yet, in predominantly Black communities traffic stops of White drivers by White officers are most likely to result in a search (Rojek, Rosenfeld, & Decker, 2012).

Despite the challenges and issues facing racial profiling research (see Engel, Calnon, & Bernard, 2002), the American public widely believes that racial profiling exists. For example, the 2004 Gallup Poll showed that slightly more than half (53%) of surveyed Americans think the practice of stopping motorists because of their race or ethnicity is "widespread." Roughly half (49%) thought racial profiling is used widely by those attempting to prevent theft in shopping malls and stores, and 42% thought that the practice is widespread at security checkpoints in airports. Not surprisingly, Blacks and Hispanics were more likely than Whites to say that profiling is widespread in these situations. It is also not a surprise that perceived racial profiling contributes to lower perceived legitimacy of police traffic stops among minorities, especially Blacks. In 2008, a quarter (25%) of Black drivers believed that the police did not have a legitimate reason for stopping them, compared to 13.7% of White and 17.5% of Hispanic drivers (Eith & Durose, 2011).

Racial/Ethnic Differences in Attitudes Toward the Police

Similar to its role in affecting street-level law enforcement, race/ ethnicity is highly relevant in determining public assessments of the police. Racial minorities, African Americans in the case of much of the research, are less inclined than Whites to display positive attitudes toward the police (Brown & Benedict, 2002; Wu et al., 2009). Studies assessing racial and ethnic attitudes suggested the existence of a "racial gradient" (Hagan et al., 2005; Portes & Rumbaut, 2001), where Whites demonstrate the most favorable attitudes toward legal authorities and Blacks the most negative, with Latinos somewhere in between (Tyler, 2001). Such a racial gradient or ladder, however, is not always successful in predicting attitudinal differences between non-Black minorities and Whites and among minority groups, implying that a single vertical scale or gradation of attitudes cannot adequately depict the complexity of distinctive racial/ethnic groups' evaluations of various aspects of policing (Wu, 2014). In this section, we briefly summarize the literature on racial differences between Blacks and Whites in their assessments of the police. In the next four chapters, we provide detailed discussion on non-Black minorities' evaluations of the police.

The majority of previous studies on race, ethnicity and attitudes toward the police have found strong evidence supporting both the sense-of-injustice and the group-position models. Early studies conducted at the request of the *President's Commission on Law Enforcement and Administration of Justice* in the 1960s found that although there was widespread satisfaction with the police, Blacks were notably less positive than Whites in their judgments of different aspects of police practice (President's Commission on Law Enforcement and Administration of Justice, 1967). Later studies have reached similar conclusions, with Blacks showing lower levels of satisfaction with or trust in the police compared to their White counterparts (e.g., Brandl, Frank, Worden, & Bynum, 1994; Carter, 1985; Dowler & Sparks, 2008; Epp et al., 2014; Huang & Vaughn, 1996; Huebner, Schafer, & Bynum, 2004; Jackson & Bradford, 2009; Jefferson & Walker, 1993; Mbuba, 2010; Miller & Davis, 2008; Murty, Roebuck, & Smith, 1990; Schuck, Rosenbaum, & Hawkins, 2008; Tyler, 2011; Wu, 2014). Researchers suggest that this difference exists because of the differential treatment of Whites and Blacks by the police, in reality or by respondents' perceptions. Research on public perceptions of racialized policing echoes this argument, revealing a shared belief across White and Black communities that police tend to treat Whites and Blacks differently (Weitzer, 2000). Further, research results can also be viewed as supporting the group position perspective. Whites have more positive views of the police because they see the police as protectors of their interests and superiority and Blacks have more negative views since they see the police as a means of controlling minority groups and maintaining the social stratification status quo.

A small number of studies, however, have shown that race has a weak or nil effect on citizens' evaluations of the police. African Americans in Detroit were actually found to exhibit more favorable views of the municipal police than did White residents in one study (Frank, Brandl, Cullen, & Stichman, 1996). The authors explained this "Detroit exception" by suggesting that a number of American cities were going through an ethno-racial political transition, which has dramatically enhanced African Americans' political influence, including the election of Black mayors and the appointment of Black police chiefs. A later replication of this study in Washington, DC, however, reached a contradictory conclusion, with African-American respondents reporting substantially lower levels of satisfaction with the police than Whites (Smith, 2005).

In addition to individual racial/ethnic background, studies have also taken neighborhood contextual variables (including racial composition) into account. Some researchers have found that the effect of race or ethnicity was not significant when various neighborhood characteristics were simultaneously considered (e.g., Cao, Frank, & Cullen, 1996; Jesilow et al., 1995; Schuman & Gruenberg, 1972). Other researchers specifically suggested that neighborhood class status played an equally important, if not greater, role than race/ethnicity in determining satisfaction with the police (Dunham & Alpert, 1988; Weitzer, 1999, 2000). Utilizing multilevel analytical modeling strategies, several studies have incorporated neighborhood racial composition (Wu et al., 2009) and concentrated disadvantage (a composite of percent Black and other social/economic indicators; see Reisig & Parks, 2003; Sampson & Jeglum-Bartusch, 1998) into analyses and found that they were both inversely related to satisfaction with the police. These results suggest that race/ethnicity is an ascribed group position in a highly stratified society, with race effects intertwined with or confounded by the effects of social class and neighborhoods.

Summary

There is no doubt that race and ethnicity have occupied and will continue to be a central theme of the U.S. policing. The lasting salience of racial discrimination and inequality in the U.S. has produced a cumulative disadvantage for the members of many racial/ethnic minority groups, disadvantages which Whites generally do not suffer. Negative racial relations foster not only unequal treatment of Black and White citizens by the police, historically and at the present time, but also differing sentiments and evaluations of the police by Black and White citizens.

Theoretical elaboration and empirical testing of subject matters related to race and policing have been accumulated over time. Researchers have contended that minorities' attitudes toward the police were chiefly influenced by their sense of being out-group members in a White-dominated society and feelings of being treated unjustly by the police. Attitudinal differences between Whites and minorities are thus attributed primarily to their varying life experiences. Official and un-official data on police arrests, use of deadly force, and traffic stops have all shown that minorities, particularly African Americans, have been subject to a heightened and disproportionate level of police interventions vis-à-vis Whites. Blacks were more likely than their White counterparts to be arrested, killed and searched during their encounters with the police. Although there is no concrete evidence supporting systematic discrimination, and some evidence suggests that the risk gap between Blacks and Whites has narrowed, the enduring racial disparity indicates that some forms of unequal treatment including that involves discrimination or bias likely remain in American policing. One of the consequences of unequal application of law enforcement is lower levels of trust and confidence in the police expressed by Blacks, compared to Whites, which reduce their willingness to cooperate with the police in the pursuit of law enforcement goals. Such reticence to partner with the police for the promotion of public safety leads to detrimental effects on community safety and social stability, for minority citizens and non-minority citizens alike. This is especially the case in many of the nation's metropolitan areas, most particularly in the urban core neighborhoods.

References

Alpert, G., Dunham, R., & Smith, M. (2007). Investigating racial profiling by the Miami-Dade Police Department: A multi-method approach. *Criminology & Public Policy, 6,* 25–55.

American Civil Liberties Union. (1999). *Driving while Black.* New York: ACLU.

Anderson, E. (1999). *Code of the streets.* New York: W. W. Norton.

Bayley, D. (1994). *Police for the future.* New York: Oxford University Press.

Belur, J. (2010). Why do the police use deadly force? Explaining police encounters in Mumbai. *British Journal of Criminology, 50,* 320–341.

Berger, J., Zelditch, M., & Anderson, B. (1972). Structural aspects of distributive justice: A status value formulation. In J. Berger, M. Zelditch, & B. Anderson (Eds.), *Sociological theories in progress* (pp. 119–146). Boston, MA: Houghton Mifflin.

Blalock, H. (1967). *Toward a theory of minority-group relations.* New York: Wiley.

Blumer, H. (1958). Race prejudice as a sense of group position. *Pacific Sociological Review, 1,* 3–7.

Bobo, L., & Hutchings, V. (1996). Perceptions of racial group competition: Extending Blumer's theory of group position to a multiracial social context. *American Sociological Review, 61,* 951–972.

Bobo, L., & Tuan, M. (2006). *Prejudice in politics: Group position, public opinion, and the Wisconsin treaty rights dispute.* Cambridge, MA: Harvard University Press.

Boydstun, J. (1975). *San Diego field interrogations: Final report.* Washington, DC: The Police Foundation.

Brame, R., Bushway, S., Paternoster, R., & Turner, M. (2014). Demographic patterns of cumulative arrest prevalence by ages 18 and 23. *Crime and Delinquency, 60,* 471–486.

Brandl, S., Frank, J., Worden, R., & Bynum, T. (1994). Global and specific attitudes toward the police: Disentangling the relationship. *Justice Quarterly, 11,* 119–134.

Brooks, L. (2001). Police discretionary behavior: A study of style. In R. Dunham & G. Alpert (Eds.), *Critical issues in policing: Contemporary reading* (pp. 117–131). Prospect Heights, IL: Waveland.

Brown, B., & Benedict, W. (2002). Perceptions of the police: Past findings, methodological issues, conceptual issues and policy implications. *Policing: An International Journal of Police Strategies and Management, 25,* 543–580.

Brown, M. (1988). *Working the street: Police discretion and the dilemmas of reform.* New York: Russell Sage Foundation.

Brown, R., & Frank, J. (2006). Race and officer decision making: Examining differences in arrest outcomes between Black and White officers. *Justice Quarterly, 23,* 96–126.

Buckler, K., & Unnever, J. (2008). Racial and ethnic perceptions of injustice: Testing the core hypotheses of comparative theory. *Journal of Criminal Justice, 36,* 270–278.

Buckler, K., Unnever, J., & Cullen, F. (2008). Perceptions of injustice revisited: A test of comparative conflict theory. *Journal of Crime and Justice, 31,* 35–57.

Cao, L., Frank, J., & Cullen, F. (1996). Race, community context and confidence in the police. *American Journal of Police, 15,* 3–22.

Carter, D. (1985). Hispanic perception of police performance: An empirical assessment. *Journal of Criminal Justice, 13,* 487–500.

Chan, J. (1997). *Changing police culture.* Cambridge, UK: Cambridge University Press.

Chideya, F. (2006). *A nation of minorities: America in 2050.* Accessed May 15, 2015 at http://www.minorityjobs.net/article/64/A-Nation-of-Minorities-America-in-2050-by-Farai-Chideya-A-Nation-of-Minorities-America-in-2050-by-Farai-Chideya.html.

Crank, J. (2004). *Understanding police culture.* Cincinnati, OH: Anderson.

Delgado, R., & Stefancic, J. (2001). *Critical race theory: An introduction.* New York: New York University Press.

Deutsch, M., & Krauss, R. (1965). *Theories in social psychology.* New York: Basic Books.

Donohue, J., & Levitt, S. (2001). The impact of race on policing and arrests. *Journal of Law and Economics, 44,* 367–394.

Dowler, K., & Sparks, R. (2008). Victimization, contact with police, and neighborhood conditions: Reconsidering African American and Hispanic attitudes toward the police. *Police Practice & Research, 9,* 395–415.

Dunham, R., & Alpert, G. (1988). Neighborhood differences in attitudes toward policing: Evidence for a mixed-strategy model of policing in a multi-ethnic setting. *Journal of Criminal Law & Criminology, 79,* 504–523.

Durose, M., Schmitt, E., & Langan, P. (2005). *Contacts between police and the public: Findings from the 2002 national survey.* Washington, DC: Bureau of Justice Statistics, US Department of Justice.

Durose, M., Smith, E., & Langan, P. (2007). *Contacts between police and the public, 2005*. Washington, DC: Bureau of Justice Statistics, US Department of Justice.

Eith, C., & Durose, M. (2011). *Contacts between police and the public, 2008*. Washington, DC: Bureau of Justice Statistics, US Department of Justice.

Eitle, D., Stolzenberg, L., & D'Alessio, S. (2005). Police organizational factors, the racial composition of the police, and the probability of arrest. *Justice Quarterly, 22*, 30–57.

Engel, R., & Calnon, J. (2004). Examining the influence of drivers' characteristics during traffic stops with police: Results from a national survey. *Justice Quarterly, 21*, 49–90.

Engel, R., Calnon, J., & Bernard, T. (2002). Theory and racial profiling: Shortcomings and future directions in research. *Justice Quarterly, 19*, 249–273.

Epp, C., Maynard-Moody, S., & Haider-Markel, D. (2014). *Pulled over: How police stops define race and citizenship*. Chicago, IL: University of Chicago Press.

Federal Bureau of Investigation. (2015). *2015 crime in the United States: Persons arrested*. Accessed January 15, 2018 at https://ucr.fbi.gov/crime-in-the-u.s/2015/crime-in-the-u.s.-2015/persons-arrested/persons arrested.

Frank, J., Brandl, S., Cullen, F., & Stichman, A. (1996). Reassessing the impact of race on citizens' attitudes toward the police: A research note. *Justice Quarterly, 13*, 321–334.

Fyfe, J. (1979). Administrative interventions on police shooting discretion: An empirical assessment. *Journal of Criminal Justice, 7*, 309–323.

Fyfe, J. (1982). Blind justice: Police shooting in Memphis. *The Journal of Criminal Law and Criminology, 73*, 707–722.

Fyfe, J. (1988). Police use of deadly force: Research and reform. *Justice Quarterly, 5*, 165–205.

Geller, W., & Scott, M. (1992). *Deadly force: What we know—A practitioner's desk-reference on police involved shootings*. Washington, DC: Police Executive Research Forum.

Green, P., & Ward, T. (2004). *State crime: Governments, violence and corruption*. London and Sterling, VA: Pluto Press.

Goldkamp, J. (1976). Minorities as victims of police shooting: Interpretations of racial disproportionality and police use of deadly force. *The Justice System Journal, 2*, 169–183.

Hacker, A. (1992). *Two nations: Black and White, separate, hostile, unequal.* New York: Macmillan.

Hagan, J., Shedd, C., & Payne, M. (2005). Race, ethnicity, and youth perceptions of criminal injustice. *American Sociological Review, 70*, 381–407.

Higginbotham, E., & Anderson, M. (2012). *Race and ethnicity in society: The changing landscape.* Belmont, CA: Wadsworth-Cengage Learning.

Higgins, G., Jennings, W., Jordan, M., & Gabbidon, S. (2011). Racial profiling in decisions to search: A preliminary analysis using propensity-score matching. *International Journal of Police Science & Management, 13*, 336–347.

Huang, W., & Vaughn, M. (1996). Support and confidence: Public attitudes toward the police. In T. Flanagan & D. Longmire (Eds.), *Americans view crime and justice: A national public opinion survey* (pp. 31–45). Thousand Oaks, CA: Sage.

Huebner, B., Schafer, J., & Bynum, T. (2004). African American and White perceptions of police services: Within- and between-group variation. *Journal of Criminal Justice, 32*, 123.

Jackson, J., & Bradford, B. (2009). Crime, policing, and social order: On the expressive nature of public confidence in policing. *British Journal of Sociology, 60*, 493–521.

Jefferson, T., & Walker, M. (1993). Attitudes to the police of ethnic minorities in a provincial city. *British Journal of Criminology, 33*, 251–266.

Jesilow, P., Meyer, J., & Namazzi, N. (1995). Public attitudes toward the police. *American Journal of the Police, 14*, 67–88.

Kochel, T., Wilson, D., & Mastrofski, S. (2011). Effect of suspect race on officers' arrest decision. *Criminology, 49*, 473–512.

LaFree, G. (1998). *Losing legitimacy: Street crime and the decline of social institutions in America.* Boulder, CO: Westview Press.

Marable, M. (1983). *How capitalism underdeveloped Black America: Problems in race, political economy, and society.* Cambridge, MA: South End Press.

Matulia, K. (1985). *A balance of forces: Model deadly force policies and procedure.* Gaithersburg, MD: International Association of Chiefs of Police.

Mbuba, J. (2010). Attitudes toward the police: The significance of race and other factors among college students. *Journal of Ethnicity in Criminal Justice, 8*, 201–215.

Meehan, A., & Ponder, M. (2002). Race and place: The ecology of racial profiling African American motorists. *Justice Quarterly, 19,* 399–430.

Meyer, M. (1980). Police shootings of minorities: The case of Los Angeles. *Annals of American Academy of Political and Social Science, 452,* 98–110.

Miller, J., & Davis, R. (2008). Unpacking public attitudes to the police: Contrasting perceptions of misconduct with traditional measures of satisfaction. *International Journal of Police Science & Management, 10,* 9–22.

Murty, K., Roebuck, J., & Smith, J. (1990). The image of the police in Black Atlanta communities. *Journal of Police Science and Administration, 17,* 20–57.

New Jersey Attorney General Office. (1999). *Interim report of the state police review team.* Accessed May 15, 2016 at http://www.state.nj.us/lps/intm_419.pdf.

New York State Commission on Criminal Justice and the Use of Force. (1987). *Report to the Governor, Vol. I.* Albany, NY: New York State Commission on Criminal Justice and the Use of Force.

Portes, A., & Rumbaut, R. (2001). *Legacies: The story of the immigrant second generation.* Berkeley, CA: University of California Press.

President's Commission on Law Enforcement and Administration of Justice. (1967). *Task force report: The police.* Washington, DC: U.S. Government Printing Office.

Reisig, M., & Parks, R. (2003). Neighborhood context, police behavior, and satisfaction with police. *Justice Research and Policy, 3,* 37–65.

Roh, S., & Robinson, M. (2009). A geographic approach to racial profiling: The microanalysis and macroanalysis of racial disparity in traffic stops. *Police Quarterly, 12,* 137–169.

Rojek, J., Rosenfeld, R., & Decker, S. (2012). Policing race: The racial stratification of searches in police traffic stops. *Criminology, 50,* 993–1024.

Runciman, G. (1966). *Relative deprivation and social justice.* London: Routledge and Kegan Paul.

Sampson, R., & Jeglum-Bartusch, D. (1998). Legal cynicism and (subcultural?) tolerance of deviance: The neighborhood context of racial differences. *Law and Society Review, 32,* 777–804.

Schafer, J., Carter, D., Katz-Bannister, A., & Wells, W. (2006). Decision-making in traffic stop encounters: A multivariate analysis of police behavior. *Police Quarterly, 9,* 184–209.

Schuck, A., Rosenbaum, D., & Hawkins, D. (2008). The influence of race/ethnicity, social class, and neighborhood context on residents' attitudes toward the police. *Police Quarterly, 11,* 496–519.

Schuman, H., & Gruenberg, B. (1972). Dissatisfaction with city services. In H. Hahn (Ed.), *People and politics in urban society* (pp. 369–392). Beverly Hill, CA: Sage.

Skolnick, J. (1966). *Justice without trial: Law enforcement in democratic society.* New York: Wiley.

Slovak, J. (1986). *Styles of urban policing.* New York: New York University Press.

Smith, B. (2005). Ethno-racial political transition and citizen satisfaction with police. *Policing: An International Journal of Police Strategies and Management, 28,* 242–254.

Smith, D., & Klein, J. (1984). Police control of interpersonal disputes. *Social Problems, 31,* 468–481.

Smith, D., & Visher, C. (1981). Street-level justice: Situational determinants of police arrest decisions. *Social Problems, 29,* 167–177.

Smith, M., & Petrocelli, M. (2001). Racial profiling? A multivariate analysis of police traffic stop data. *Police Quarterly, 4,* 4–27.

Snyder, H. (2011). *Arrest in the United States, 1980–2009.* Washington, DC: Bureau of Justice Statistics, U.S. Department of Justice.

Spano, R. (2003). Concerns about safety, observer sex, and the decision to arrest: Evidence of reactivity in a large scale observational study of police. *Criminology, 41,* 909–932.

Sullivan, J. (1992, May 11). New Jersey panel urges uniform guidelines for police use of deadly force. *The New York Times,* p. A13.

Sun, I. (2003). Police officers' attitudes toward their role and work: A comparison between Black and White officers. *American Journal of Criminal Justice, 28,* 89–108.

Sun, I., & Payne, B. (2004). Racial differences in resolving conflicts: A comparison between Black and White police officers. *Crime and Delinquency, 50,* 516–541.

Sun, I., Payne, B., & Wu, Y. (2008). The impact of situational, officer, and neighborhood characteristics on police behavior: A multilevel analysis. *Journal of Criminal Justice, 36,* 22–32.

Takagi, P. (1974). A garrison state in 'democratic' society. *Crime and Social Justice, 1,* 27–33.

Tennenbaum, A. (1994). The influence of the garner decision on police use of deadly force. *Journal of Criminal Law & Criminology, 85,* 241–260.

Tyler, T. (1990). *Why people obey and law.* New Haven, CT: Yale University Press.

Tyler, T. (2001). Public trust and confidence in legal authorities: What do majority and minority group members want from the law and legal authorities? *Behavioral Sciences & the Law, 19,* 215–235.

Tyler, T. (2003). Procedural justice, legitimacy, and the effective rule of law. In M. Tonry (Ed.), *Crime and justice: A review of research* (pp. 283–357). Chicago, IL: University of Chicago Press.

Tyler, T. (2011). Trust and legitimacy: Policing in the USA and Europe. *European Journal of Criminology, 8,* 254–266.

Walker, S., & Katz, C. (2013). *The police in America: An introduction.* New York: McGraw-Hill.

Walker, S., Spohn, S., & Delone, M. (2003). *The color of justice: Race, ethnicity and crime in America.* Belmont, CA: Wadsworth-Cengage Learning.

Warren, P., Tomaskovic-Devey, D., Smith, W., Zingraff, M., & Mason, M. (2006). Driving while Black: Bias processes and racial disparity in police stops. *Criminology, 44,* 709–738.

Weitzer, R. (1999). Citizens' perceptions of police misconduct: Race and neighborhood context. *Justice Quarterly, 16,* 819–846.

Weitzer, R. (2000). Racialized policing: Residents' perceptions in three neighborhoods. *Law and Society Review, 34,* 129–155.

Weitzer, R., & Tuch, S. (2005). Racially biased policing: Determinants of citizen perceptions. *Social Forces, 83,* 1009–1030.

Weitzer, R., & Tuch, S. (2006). *Race and policing in America: Conflict and reform.* New York: Cambridge University Press.

White, M. (2002). Identifying situational predictors of police shooting using multivariate analysis. *Policing: An International Journal of Police Strategies and Management, 25,* 726–751.

Willits, D., & Nowacki, J. (2014). Police organisation and deadly force: An examination of variation across large and small cities. *Policing and Society, 24,* 63–80.

Wilson, W. (1987). *The declining significance of race.* Chicago, IL: University of Chicago Press.

Withrow, B. (2004). Race-based policing: A descriptive analysis of the Wichita Stop Study. *Police Practice and Research, 5,* 223–240.

Worden, R. (1989). Situational and attitudinal explanations of police behavior: A theoretical reappraisal and empirical assessment. *Law and Society Review, 23,* 667–711.

Worden, R. (1996). The causes of police brutality: Theory and evidence on police use of force. In W. Geller & H. Toch (Eds.), *Police violence: Understanding and controlling police abuse of force* (pp. 23–51). New Haven, CT: Yale University Press.

Wu, Y. (2014). Race/ethnicity and perceptions of the police: A comparison of White, Black, Asian and Hispanic Americans. *Policing and Society, 24,* 135–157.

Wu, Y., Sun, I., & Triplett, R. (2009). Race, class or neighborhood context: Which matters more in measuring satisfaction with police? *Justice Quarterly, 26,* 125–156.

Cases Cited

Terry v. Ohio, 392 U.S. 1 (1968).
Whren et al. v. United States, 517 U.S. 806 (1996).

3

Policing the Country's Newcomers

Historically, in the U.S. there have been numerous periods in which immigrants have been viewed as culturally incompatible and physically too different from "real Americans" so that their presence in large numbers constituted a genuine problem for the nation (Stockwell, 1927). The police at all levels of government have historically collectively shouldered the responsibility of enforcing the country's immigration and criminal laws and local government ordinances and public policies enacted to control such immigrant populations, be they the Irish, the German, the Polish, or—in more recent decades, the Asian, African and Latin American immigrants. Though U.S. immigration law enforcement traditionally within the bailiwick of the federal government, state and local policing policies, strategies and tactics arguably have the most influential and most direct impact on the perceptions and developing expectations of new arrivals in this country. Not unexpectedly, then, much historical research has documented strained relations between the police and a variety of immigrant groups settling in the U.S. Quite often serious ongoing tensions, both overt and more subtle types of discrimination, and persisting differential treatment are experienced by immigrants at the hands of local police. The history of U.S. policing

© The Author(s) 2018
I. Y. Sun and Y. Wu, *Race, Immigration, and Social Control*,
Palgrave Studies in Race, Ethnicity, Indigeneity and Criminal Justice,
https://doi.org/10.1057/978-1-349-95807-8_3

is indeed filled with examples of troubling and oftentimes long-lasting conflict between local police and various immigrant minority groups (Walker, 1998).

This chapter first discusses the ideologies, beliefs and theories that underline social control strategies toward immigrants developed in the U.S. The chapter also depicts how a variety of immigrant groups were treated and policed historically, and clarifies the complex connection obtaining between immigrant groups and their records of criminal offending. The chapter then delineates challenges faced by the police in establishing and maintaining public order among and protecting an increasingly diverse immigrant population before the 9/11 terrorist attacks. Finally, the chapter focuses on emerging challenges in immigration and law enforcement in the era of post-9/11 policing in the U.S.

Keeping Them at Bay: Taming Immigrant Enclaves

The U.S. is a country established by immigrants, and one to which immigration waves came as the nation grew geographically and in global influence. Over the past four centuries, the country has experienced successive great waves of immigration, starting with settlers from different segments of Western Europe and Eastern Europe to newcomers from Latin America, Asia and Africa. Although a generally open door policy that welcomed nearly all immigrants to the New World was gradually replaced with a much more restrictive one, the ongoing entry of ethnically and culturally distinct groups and their geographic concentration in particular areas created a great many immigrant *enclaves* throughout the country (Logan, Zhang, & Alba, 2002). Such ethnic communities historically have been, and continue to this day, to serve as safe havens for recently arrived immigrants to locate temporary housing and secure employment and lay stepping stones to their assimilation into America society. Extended living and working in such immigrant enclaves, however, could prolong the adaptation and assimilation process, and be more broadly viewed by long-time residents as an intentional inflammatory refusal to join the mainstream of American society.

Supporters of restrictive federal immigration laws and associated state and local policies often contend that immigration should be limited in scope in as much as they are unaccustomed to our ways and create competition for resources, public services, and employment for current citizens. Directly pertinent to the field of crime and justice, some researchers have posited that the close regulation of immigration and the careful watch kept over immigrants have arisen primarily because of the threatening image of immigrant criminality (Chacón, 2007). Due to the cultural and racial distinctiveness of so many newcomers, particularly those who are undocumented, they are often portrayed in media as aggressive and violent gang members, drug dealers, and violent criminals who are responsible for a large share of crimes being committed in our society (Ferguson, 2008).

The stereotypes related to the perceived threat and/or adverse impact of foreign-born persons and their progeny are particularly strongly held with respect to Latino immigrants (Timberlake, Howell, Grau, & Williams, 2015). Furthermore, negative public perceptions of immigrant criminality went beyond considerations of elevated crime rates in and about immigrant enclaves; those perceptions were also shaped in part by high-profile violent crime incidents involving undocumented immigrants (Sohoni & Sohoni, 2014). Despite the lack of evidence supporting a concrete link between immigration and crime (Sampson, 2008), the presumptively crime-enhancing effect of immigration has surfaced repeatedly during public debates and reached the pinnacle recently when then-2016 presidential candidate Donald Trump on multiple occasions referred to Mexican immigrants as criminals and rapists who would be "gone on day one" should he be elected and sworn into office.

With respect to the academic literature, there is a long history of portrayal of a close relationship between immigrant status and criminal conduct. Children of immigrant families have been instrumental in the early development of criminological theories given their uncommon existence straddling two cultures and being marginalized within the prevailing economic and social status systems. For example, relying heavily upon data from juvenile immigrants residing in Chicago neighborhoods, the proponents of social disorganization theory noted that adverse structural characteristics, such as poverty, residential mobility and racial heterogeneity, were accompanied with high degrees of social disorganization in transitional communities. This disorganization in turn led to high rates of crime and delinquency (Shaw & McKay, 1942). Specifically, newly arrived immigrants were most likely to settle within highly unstable, high turnover Chicago neighborhoods where the collective capability of residents in establishing common values and exercising effective informal control to intervene in and solve common problems was weak. The weakness of informal control allowed deviant and criminal behavior to flourish. In addition to residing in neighborhoods with high degrees of structural and organizational disadvantages, lower-class immigrant youth generally lacked access to legitimate opportunities to succeed. Such opportunities being lacking, the formation of subcultures entailing high risk and high gain criminal behavior offered an attractive alternative to low-paying employment in dead-end jobs (Cloward & Ohlin, 1960).

In addition to concerns about immigrants' involvement in criminal offending, another major argument made in behalf of strictly controlling the character of immigration entails the "economic threat" posed by immigrants for some sectors of the domestic economy. Immigrants are widely seen as competitors for employment opportunities (Johnson, 2004). Although there is little evidence indicating a close linkage between immigrant labor availability and unemployment rates of native-born workers (unskilled immigrants mainly work in sectors of the workforce which do not attract native-born persons), immigrants are often blamed for taking jobs from citizens. This claim is particularly appealing to many economically marginalized persons during economic recessions when unemployment is high. Undocumented workers are also accused of driving average wages down and using public services and resources without paying their fair share of taxes. It is often the case, in this regard, that unscrupulous employers frequently exploit unauthorized workers by paying them less than the minimum wage and without the provision of health and retirement benefits.

One of the most common myths perpetuated about immigration is its supposed impact on the incidence of crime. Research has failed to provide consistent and strong evidence to support an immigrant-crime nexus; instead, there is growing evidence suggesting protective effects of immigration. Based on official arrest and incarceration statistics or on case studies of gangs/crime groups, prior studies have mostly focused on the effect of foreign-born-status on violent offending. At the aggregate level (e.g., within neighborhoods, cities, regional areas, states, and nations), the majority of past studies have shown either a weak or no association between immigrant population and the rate of crime and incarceration (e.g., Diaz, 2011). During the period 1990–2010, the levels of immigration and crime in the U.S. were **inversely related**, with the percentage of foreign-born showing an upward trend while crime rates were displaying a downward tendency. Indeed, the influx of immigrants could contribute to the decline of crime rates by raising the denominator while not significantly changing the numerator.

At the state level, states with a higher percentage of foreign-born did not experience a higher crime rate. Table 3.1 displays violent and property crime rates in 10 U.S. states with the highest percentages of foreign-born populations. With the exception of Nevada, **none** of the top 10 immigrant states were ranked on the top 10 most violent places in the U.S. The ranking for property crimes shows a similar pattern— that is, the top immigrant settlement states were not ranked on the top

Table 3.1 Percentage of foreign-born and crime rate in top U.S. immigrant states, 2015

State	Percentage of foreign-born[a]		Crime rate[b] (per 100,000 inhabitants)			
	%	Rank[c]	Violent	Rank[c]	Property	Rank[c]
California	27.1	1	426.3	13	2668.3	21
New York	22.6	2	379.7	23	1604.0	48
New Jersey	21.2	3	255.4	38	1626.5	47
Florida	19.4	4	461.9	11	2813.2	17
Nevada	19.2	5	695.9	1	2668.3	21
Hawaii	18.1	6	293.4	31	3796.2	1
Texas	16.4	7	412.2	16	2831.3	15
Massachusetts	15.0	8	390.9	18	1690.7	46
Maryland	14.3	9	457.2	12	2315.0	27
Connecticut	13.8	10	218.5	45	1812.0	42

[a]U.S. Census data
[b]FBI UCR data
[c]Rank among all 50 U.S. states

10 list of property crime, with the sole exception of Hawaii. Within metropolitan areas, immigrant settlement was also consistently associated with **decreases** in both violent and property crimes (Adelman, Reid, Markle, Weiss, & Jaret, 2017; Stowell, Messner, McGeever, & Raffalovich, 2009). Analyses of data from individual cities, such as Chicago, Los Angeles, and San Diego, also revealed a negative correlation between immigration and crime rates (MacDonlad, Hipp, & Gill, 2013; Martinez, Stowell, & Iwama, 2016; Sampson, 2008).

At the individual level, the foreign-born population is not more crime prone than their native-born counterparts, but second-generation immigrants are likely to catch up to U.S.-born persons in their rate of criminal activity (Bersani, 2014). Looking at specific immigrant groups, foreign-born Hispanic youth are less inclined than their native-born counterparts to engage in criminal offending, and this pattern holds for various Hispanic subgroups (Lopez & Miller, 2011; Miller, 2012). Another study found that, with the exception of Hispanic immigrants, the foreign-born populations from Asia, Africa and Europe reported a lower prevalence of intimate partner violence than native-born Americans (Vaughn, Salas-Wright, Cooper-Sadlo, Maynard, & Larson, 2015).

Notwithstanding lack of empirical support for the stigmatic link between immigrants and crime, among law enforcement cross the board it is fair to say that immigration enforcement and law enforcement have geared their activities primarily toward the regulation of legally resident aliens and undocumented foreigners. Indeed, the regulation of immigration has been historically carried out through the regulatory actions of the federal government's U.S. Border Patrol, and post-entry social control exercised by a combination of civil society and state and local government actions. A large part of internal enforcement of the immigration laws has taken placed through deportation. Although deportation has been treated as a civil matter by the U.S. courts, removal from U.S. territory constitutes a punishment that has raised serious questions about fundamental fairness and due process of law (Kanstroom, 2000). In recent decades, the convergence of deportation and crime control has been observed, with the criminal justice system being increasingly employed to sanction and control immigration violations

(Provine, Varsanyi, Lewis, & Decker, 2016). The intersection of and shifts between policing and deportation have made immigrants and other marginalized cultural groups more vulnerable to social control (Rosenbloom, 2016).

The 9/11 terrorist attacks have further pushed immigration enforcement to focus squarely on criminal enforcement, with the several boundaries between immigration enforcement, crime control and national security becoming highly blurred (Chacón, 2007). Immigrants are extremely defenseless to immigration and criminal enforcement as they are entitled to fewer constitutional protections than citizens and the intertwined and overlapping nature of federal, state and local agencies somewhat obfuscates and complicates the attainment of accountability in enforcement. The next section of this chapter discusses the intertwined nature of immigration and criminal control before and after the 9/11 attacks, highlighting critical developments and events that have shaped and reshaped the dynamics of policing immigrant communities.

Policing Increasingly Diverse Immigrant Communities Before 9/11

Over the past three centuries, Colonial America and the U.S. have received millions of immigrants from first Western Europe and Africa (as slaves), then from Northern, Southern and Eastern Europe, and later from Latin America and Asia. Over the course of this entire history, the negative stereotype of immigrants as an imminent threat to the established social order of mainstream society has been present. Each major wave of immigration spurred shockwaves of anti-immigrant sentiments and the adoption of anti-immigrant policies. Quite naturally, law enforcement officers became intimately involved in the enforcement of these policies. For example, during the second half of the nineteenth century many Chinese workers were systematically driven out from their communities by treacherous politicians and lawless citizens (Pfaelzer, 2007). The anti-Chinese resentment reached its peak in 1882 when the U.S. Congress passed the *Chinese Exclusion Act*, a statute prohibiting all immigration of Chinese laborers (see Chapter 5 for more detailed discussion of the history of Chinese immigration to the U.S.).

The legal system in general, and the police in particular, was charged with dealing with many violent vigilante attacks upon Chinese immigrant workers in California and other states in the U.S. West. County Sheriff offices were responsible for collecting discriminatory taxes from Chinese workers (McClain, 1994), and many police officers received regular payoffs (bribes) in exchange for protecting illegal gambling and prostitution establishment in Chinatowns in San Francisco and Los Angeles (Tsai, 1986).

In addition to these injustices done to Chinese workers in the U.S. West, violence and discrimination against other Asian immigrant groups in California, Oregon and Washington such as Japanese and Filipinos have been well documented by historians (Lee, 2007). Another large foreign-born group, Mexican immigrants, has endured similar racism and state violence in the second half of the nineteenth century (Chacón & Davis, 2006) (see Chapter 4 for more discussion of violence perpetrated against Latino immigrants). Even white ethnic immigrant workers were not immune from mob violence by the dominant Anglo Saxon population in Pennsylvania and West Virginia, although their experiences of violence and expulsion were less severe and somewhat less systematic as that experienced by Asian and Mexican immigrants (Diaz, 2011). Despite the history of persistent animosity being shown toward newcomers to America, a large number of unskilled foreigners continued to arrive and settle in dilapidated and crowded areas within the nation's major gateway cities. There they take up any menial jobs available as has occurred over the course of American settlement, and they often experience a tumultuous process of acculturation while simultaneously enduring economic hardship until finding their niche in American society (Portes & Manning, 2008). Sadly enough, American policing practice during this long period of ongoing immigration to the U.S. was characterized as largely inefficient, too often corrupt, and entirely susceptible to political influence (Kelling & Moore, 1988).

In the early twentieth century, some northern states utilized the temperance and prohibition social movements to moderate the influx of immigrant groups coming into their states. The prohibition against possession, sale and production of alcohol was weakly enforced in most jurisdictions, a fact which not only led organized crime to flourish after gaining control over the lucrative black market but also occasioned widespread corruption among law enforcement and other government agencies. One of the largest and most well-known bootleggers in the Pacific Northwest region was Roy Olmstead, who was a former Lieutenant with the Seattle Police Department. Olmstead engaged in bootlegging while still serving as a police officer, and he was personally involved in many raids and arrests of bootleggers who were not part of his own operation (McClary, 2002).

During the four decades following World War II the United States witnessed an increase in immigration equivalent to the level experienced at the beginning of the century. In addition to low-wage, unskilled laborers, who comprised most of the immigrants before World War I, after World War II hundreds of thousands of foreigners who were professionals, technicians, and highly skilled craftsmen migrated to the U.S. under the *Immigration Act of 1965*. This group of better trained and occupationally skilled immigrants tended to scatter around the country rather than concentrating in ethnic enclaves within urban settings (Portes & Manning, 2008). Since the 1960s, many urban communities also underwent rapid demographic transformations, with long-time inner city residents moving to suburbs in droves while immigrants from Latin American and Asian countries settling in urban core city neighborhoods.

The post-World War II decades represented the most challenging era of U.S. policing; law enforcement agencies faced an increasingly complex and demanding working environment featuring the influx of diverse immigrant and minority groups into cities, the skyrocketing of crime and disorder, the struggle of the civil rights movement, the widespread protests of the unpopular Vietnam war, and the increased oversight of police actions by the courts. Although American law enforcement has gradually evolved from political to professional organizations emphasizing centralization, professionalism, and widespread use of information and communication technology, a crime fighting-centered strategy continued to guide police thinking. That strategy featured aggressive patrol interventions and use of resources primarily to reduce "response time" to crimes reported to police. These priorities served to isolate the police from the public and created strained relations, particularly with minority and immigrant communities living in high-crime areas featuring concentrated poverty (Kelling & Moore, 1988).

In due course most American police departments came to adopt the model of community policing as an organizational survival strategy to address increasingly poor police-minority community relations occasioned by heavy reliance on the professional style of policing described above. With an emphasis on bridging the divide that had previously alienated police from their communities, community policing empowered front-line officers with greater flexibility and autonomy to cultivate closer ties with local residents.

Community policing, while a more appropriate approach to policing in a pluralistic and highly diverse society, nonetheless entails many different strategies and programs in different departments. Some agencies stress use of traditional aggressive enforcement strategies (e.g., traffic and suspicion stops, drug enforcement, and arrests) to enhance the quality of life in the high crime neighborhoods, whereas others emphasize the use of collaborative problem-solving approaches to improve police service and citizen satisfaction across the board. While much progress has been made toward implementing community policing across the country, noteworthy pockets of resistance to reform remain. The constant concern for crime and public safety, and rhetoric associated with the War on Drugs, have kept many departments wedded to aggressive and even abusive practices such as racial profiling and use of specialized units making use of asset seizure and forfeiture accompanying drug raids as a major portion of agency revenue. While such an approach may add substantially to the amassing of record levels of arrest, drug busts, and assets seized from illicit activities, it results in the tarnishing of the public image of their police and brings into question their genuine effectiveness, fairness and integrity.

Using New York City to elucidate, under the Giuliani Administration the NYPD launched the so-called program of *zero-tolerance policing* in 1994 focusing on the vigorous suppression of minor offenses and disorders, following a "broken windows" conception of law enforcement popularized by James Q. Wilson and George Kelling (1982). This was done in the hopes of preventing minor disorders from escalating into more serious problems leading to the commission of serious crimes. A clear "law and order" narrative was developed and promoted to highlight the widespread problem of infrastructure deterioration in many neighborhoods and the urgent necessity for rebuilding the image of the city through the reduction of crime and enhancement of social control (Lindsey, 2004). Patrol officers constantly engaged in "quality of life" measures on the street, and NYPD's notorious Street Crimes Unit (SCU) patrolled high crime neighborhoods in unmarked cars and often swooped down on suspicious individuals for possible crime in progress or suspicious criminal activity (Lindsey, 2004).

Not surprisingly, the reality of aggressive social control has a disproportionate negative impact on minority neighborhoods commonly featuring a large representation of immigrants; it was too often these immigrants who became the victims of police brutality. Two high-profile cases occurred in the 1990s which serve as illustrative examples. In 1997, the police in Brooklyn arrested Haitian immigrant Abner Louima outside a nightclub for assaulting an officer and resisting arrest. Louima was taken to the police station where he was beaten and brutally sodomized by police officers. Two officers were found guilty of assault and perjury charges. In 1999, the deadly shooting of Amadou Diallo, a young immigrant from Guinea, stirred even greater scrutiny for possible racially-biased policing exercised by NYPD. Suspecting Diallo as a serial rapist, four SCU plain-clothes officers in Bronx fired a total of 41 shots when they saw Diallo reaching into his pocket for an object, which turned out to be his wallet. The SCU was eventually disbanded, but the four officers involved in the shooting were acquitted of all criminal charges.

The problem of racial profiling surfaced around the nation in the 1990s, signaling that biased social control and the abusive War on Drugs were taking a heavy and unequal toll on minority and immigrant communities.

In addition to traffic stops and subsequent searches involving a disproportionate percentage of black drivers and, to a lesser extent, Latino motorists, immigration enforcement is similarly driven by race and ethnicity (see Chapter 2 for more discussion on racial disparity on traffic stops). Indeed, racialized immigration raids, workplace sweeps and random citizenship checks were common policing tactics used to control and reinforce subordinated status among working-class Latino immigrants and Latino citizens (Romero, 2006).

An excellent example of racialized immigration enforcement is the "Chandler Roundup," an event which took place in Chandler, Arizona in 1997 as a joint operation by local and federal law enforcement authorities. Hundreds of suspected undocumented immigrants, almost exclusively Latino, were arrested and later deported. During the five-day operation, however, many Latino American citizens and legal residents were also stopped and arrested mainly because of their skin color and Latino appearance, causing an ordeal of embarrassment, humiliation and fear. A critic of such actions has asserted the following: "Immigration policing constructed citizenship as visibly inscribed on bodies in specific urban spaces rather than probable cause" (Romero, 2006, p. 447).

The 9/11 attacks in 2001 brought up new challenges to policing immigrant populations in the U.S. Under the foremost concern of homeland security, the country has become increasingly restrictive in permitting immigration entry and selective in targeting foreign groups. When counterterrorism claims the top spot on the national security agenda, immigration enforcement once again serves as one of the key policing functions—namely, to ensure effective control over high-risk out-groups.

Surfacing Challenges in the Post-9/11 Era of Policing

The September 11, 2001 tragedy has had a substantial impact on a great many segments in American society. Looking at the nation's law enforcement community, counterterrorism has clearly emerged as one of the top priorities in the post-9/11 era of American policing. An expanded role of police organizations in homeland security generally, and in anti-terrorism, intelligence-gathering, and immigration law enforcement particularly has been widely observed. The term "the widened criminal justice model" was used to depict those organizational and operational changes that deviate from traditional police practices, such as the creation of specialized counterterrorism and intelligence units and the incorporation of anti-terrorism strategies and tactics in police training (Greene & Herzog, 2009).

Besides law enforcement officers, another group of people that has been deeply influenced by the 9/11 attacks is Arab immigrants and American citizens of Arab descent. They have become the primary targets of post-9/11 investigations. Indeed, the 9/11 events have forever transformed popular discourse on Arab Americans from that of "invisible citizens" to that of "highly visible subjects" (Jamal & Naber, 2008). The aftermath of the horrific events, such as the War on Terror, the heightened public suspicion of Arab immigrants and Arab Americans as potential terrorists, the political and economic backlash and hate crimes against Arab people and their community organizations, and the increased role of local police agencies in intelligence gathering and immigration law enforcement, has generated a "special relationship" between Arab Americans and immigrants, law enforcement agencies, and the media (Howell & Jamal, 2009). When immigrant status intersects with ethnicity and nationality, as it does in the area of national security, both Arab Americans/immigrants and local police departments have to overcome extra barriers to construct positive relations (see Chapter 6 for more detailed discussion on the issue).

Immediately after the 9/11 attacks, the Federal Bureau of Investigation (FBI) and local law enforcement authorities questioned and arrested hundreds of Arab men mainly for expired visitor or student visas (Bryan, 2005). Attorney General Ashcroft ordered the FBI to interview five-thousand Arab and/or Muslim men who were in the country on temporary visas in order to gather potentially useful information for use in the War on Terror. The intrusive nature of the questions asked made the voluntary nature of these interviews widely questioned. Some law enforcement officials expressed their concerns about the negative effect of these information-gathering interviews on the relationship between police departments and Arab immigrant groups.

Under heightened concerns about terrorist attacks carried out by foreign nationals, state and local police departments faced increasing demands for carrying out immigration law enforcement, an essential and traditional role of federal agencies (Provine et al., 2016). Perhaps one of the most notorious local law enforcement officials in policing immigrants is Joe Arpaio, Sheriff of Maricopa County, Arizona. Known widely as "America's toughest sheriff," Sheriff Arpaio and his deputies started very aggressively enforcing immigration laws in 2005 through the use of "saturation patrols" and un-announced immigration sweeps, targeting almost exclusively Latino day laborers and residents in Latino-concentrated local neighborhoods. The department formed an immigrant smuggling squad to stop vehicles with Latino drivers and/or passengers and carry out inspections of their immigration status. Aggressive immigration enforcement also extended to conducting many routine traffic stops and conducting searches when suspicion of wrongdoing was present and busting in on local businesses and arresting Latino employees who were undocumented. Surveillance cameras covering public spaces were widely employed in Maricopa county municipalities to deter undocumented immigrants from making use of those public places (McDowall & Wonders, 2009).

Arizona's strong anti-immigration policy was crystalized in the state's passage of the *Support Our Law Enforcement and Safe Neighborhoods Act* in 2011, commonly known as Arizona Senate Bill 1070 (SB 1070). The notorious statute requires state and local law enforcement officers to, among other things, ascertain an individual's immigration status during any traffic/suspicious activity stop, detention or arrest if the officer suspects that person might be undocumented. If suspicions persist, the officer must detain the individual and contact federal immigration authorities. The principal idea behind the adoption of SB 1070 is **attrition through enforcement** (Vaughan, 2006). That is, if regulatory authorities can make the daily lives of undocumented immigrants difficult enough through aggressive enforcement, then immigrants are likely to voluntarily "self-deport"—that is, return to their home countries (Theodore, 2011).

Deeply concerned about potential civil rights violations, the U.S. Department of Justice filed a lawsuit against the State of Arizona in 2010, and in 2012 the Supreme Court ruled against several clauses of the law that allow police officers to arrest without a warrant in some situations, make it a misdemeanor for an immigrant who fails to carry documentation of lawful presence in the country, and render it unlawful for a person to apply for employment without federal work authorization. The Court, however, also upheld the part of the law that allows Arizona police to investigate the immigration status of an individual stopped, detained, or arrested if there is reasonable suspicion that the person is in the country without proper documentation.

The Supreme Court ruling on SB 1070 has essentially expanded the influence of state and local police agencies on immigration enforcement by permitting them to blend border control techniques with domestic policing tactics and mix administrative and criminal approaches to stop, apprehend, and deport unauthorized immigrants (Provine & Sanchez, 2011). Apparently, the criminal justice system has gradually surfaced as a primary means for monitoring, regulating and criminalizing non-citizens, documented and undocumented, a phenomenon that has been referred to as **crimmigration** (Chacón, 2009; Stumpf, 2006). Thus far, the involvement of local police in federal immigration enforcement has yet to yield any measurable and noteworthy public safety benefits (Treyger, Chalfin, & Loeffler, 2014).

The controversial Joe Arpaio lost his re-election bid in November, 2016, but announced to run for Senate in January 2018. Arpaio was surely not the only county sheriff who was eager to take immigration control into his own hands. The chief federal immigration enforcement agency, U.S. Immigration and Custom Enforcement (ICE), has a 287(g) program that officially empowers state and local law enforcement agencies with the authority for immigration enforcement within their jurisdictions. As of March 2017, 37 law enforcement agencies in 16 states are 287(g) program participants, with the majority of them being county sheriff offices. Albeit still small in participation rate among all sheriff offices, and reflecting somewhat of a downward trend in 287(g) partner number since 2011 (Rhodan, 2017, April 3), the program is highly likely to see new life as the Trump administration has proclaimed its preference for a much more stringent policy toward undocumented immigrants and a desire to witness far more extensive participation by local police in immigration law enforcement.

Public disappointment with the federal government's failure to enact meaningful immigration reform and the periodic occurrence of high profile violent attacks involving unauthorized immigrants have combined to enhance anti-immigrant sentiment and placed local police departments under mounting pressure to act. Nevertheless, local police have been highly cautious in enforcing immigration laws as it is likely to generate distrust of the police, threatening police-immigrant community relations and lowering immigrants' willingness to cooperate with the local police. The intertwined nature of the demand of stronger immigration control and the concern about negative consequence of aggressive enforcement has created some dilemmas, and even led to the existence of contradictory policies and policing activities in many police departments in many of our states (Johnson, 2004).

In Nashville, Kentucky, for example, the police launched a community policing program aimed at enhancing communication and trust with Latino immigrant residents, while patrol officers undermined such efforts to build trust and cooperation by ticketing and arresting Latino residents who were unable to present a state-issued ID (Armenta, 2016). In Palisades Park, New Jersey, despite suffering from a high degree of victimization, undocumented migrant workers were highly unlikely to report their victimizations to the police, but they were keen to contact the police to seek assistance and information in non-legal contexts (Sung, Delgado, Peña, & Paladino, 2016). This suggests that although migrant workers are trustful of the police in protecting and serving, they are more fearful of the police for detecting and reporting their immigration status to immigration authorities, to the extent of being willing to put their own lives and property in danger.

Summary

As a country populated by immigrants from across the world attracted to the "Land of Opportunity," the U.S. has a long history of both welcoming immigration and then seeking to control its most recent immigrant populations through laws, regulations and policies and, at various times, tolerating the use of vigilante violence and state collective violence in exerting its will over immigrant groups. Public debates on immigration have spurred greater attention to the social costs and consequences associated with immigration, such as employment, education, social welfare, and the most notably, the incidence of crime. A common myth associated with immigration debates is that immigrants tend to commit more crimes than citizens, which has received little if any support in systematic research on the immigration-crime connection.

The stereotype of immigrants as cultural, economic and political threats to social stability has led to waves of extreme anti-immigration sentiments in the nineteenth century and the twentieth century, times during which police officers were inevitably involved as enforcers of often unjust and draconian laws. Violence against Asian immigrant groups, including Chinese, Japanese, and Filipinos in California and Latinos in the American Southwest, for example, were intentionally ignored by law enforcement officers. In recent decades, in the name of law and order and a "War on Drugs," aggressive enforcement carried out by many police agencies observes problems of discriminatory profiling and unfair controlling of minority groups, including immigrant populations.

The events of 9/11 terrorist attacks have further posed challenges to maintaining positive police-immigrant community relations, with people of Arab descent particularly becoming primary targets of the post-9/11 Homeland Security investigation. State and local police departments, under the current conservative political environment, have also faced progressively onerous demands for performing immigration law enforcement in connection with national security. When the lines between civil and criminal immigration consequences are increasingly blurred, crimmigration inevitably occurs and state and local police agencies often find themselves struggling with exercising sensitive and fair policing. How to achieve the goal of effective crime control without scarifying the fundamental principles of fairness, integrity and accountability has most certainly remained one of the toughest challenges facing policing in America.

References

Adelman, R., Reid, L., Markle, G., Weiss, S., & Jaret, C. (2017). Urban crime rates and the changing face of immigration: Evidence across four decades. *Journal of Ethnicity in Criminal Justice, 15*, 52–77.

Armenta, A. (2016). Between public service and social control: Policing dilemmas in the era of immigration enforcement. *Social Problems, 63*, 111–126.

Bersani, B. (2014). An examination of first and second generation immigrant offending trajectories. *Justice Quarterly, 31*, 315–343.

Bryan, J. (2005). Constructing "the true Islam" in hostile times: The impact of 9/11 on Arab Muslims in Jersey City. In N. Foner (Ed.), *Wounded city: The social impact of 9/11* (pp. 133–159). New York: Russell Sage Foundation.

Chacón, J. (2007). Unsecured borders: Immigration restrictions, crime control and national security. *Connecticut Law Review, 39*, 1827–1891.

Chacón, J. (2009). Managing migration through crime. *Columbia Law Review Sidebar, 109*, 135–148.

Chacón, J., & Davis, M. (2006). *No one is illegal: Fighting racism and state violence on the U.S.-Mexico border*. Chicago, IL: Haymarket Books.

Cloward, R., & Ohlin, L. (1960). *Delinquency and opportunity: A theory of delinquent gangs*. Glencoe, IL: Free Press.

Diaz, J. (2011). Immigration policy, criminalization and the growth of the immigration industrial complex: Restriction, expulsion and eradication of undocumented in the U.S. *Western Criminological Review, 12*, 35–54.

Ferguson, C. (2008). Portrayals of immigrants in mass media: Honest depiction of cultural differences or unfair stereotype? In J. Warner (Ed.), *Battleground immigration* (Vol. 1). Westport, CT: Greenwood.

Greene, J., & Herzog, S. (2009). The implications of terrorism on the formal and social organization of policing in the U.S. and Israel: Some concerns and opportunities. In D. Weisburd, T. Feucht, I. Hakimi, L. Mock, & S. Perry (Eds.), *To protect and to serve: Policing in an age of terrorism* (pp. 143–175). New York: Springer.

Howell, S., & Jamal, A. (2009). The aftermath of the 9/11 attacks. In Detroit Arab American Study Team (Eds.), *Citizenship and crisis: Arab Detroit after 9/11* (pp. 69–100). New York: Russell Sage Foundation.

Jamal, A., & Naber, N. (Eds.). (2008). *Race and Arab Americans before and after 9/11: From invisible citizens to visible subjects*. Syracuse, NY: Syracuse University Press.

Johnson, K. (2004). *The huddled masses myth: Immigration and civil rights.* Philadelphia, PA: Temple University Press.

Kanstroom, D. (2000). Deportation, social control and punishment: Some thoughts about why hard laws make bad cases. *Harvard Law Review, 113,* 1890–1935.

Kelling, G., & Moore, M. (1988). From political reform to community: The evolving strategy of police. In J. Greene & S. Mastrofski (Eds.), *Community policing: Rhetoric or reality* (pp. 3–25). New York: Praeger.

Lee, E. (2007). The "Yellow Peril" and Asian exclusion in the Americas. *Pacific Historical Review, 76,* 537–562.

Lindsey, D. (2004). To build a more 'perfect discipline': Ideologies of the normative and the social control of the criminal innocent in the policing of New York City. *Critical Sociology, 30,* 321–353.

Logan, J., Zhang, W., & Alba, R. (2002). Immigrant enclaves and ethnic communities in New York and Los Angeles. *American Sociological Review, 67,* 299–322.

Lopez, K., & Miller, H. (2011). Ethnicity, acculturation, and offending: Findings from a sample of Hispanic adolescents. *The Open Family Studies Journal, 4,* 27–37.

MacDonlad, J., Hipp, J., & Gill, C. (2013). The effects of immigrant concentration on changes in neighborhood crime rates. *Journal of Quantitative Criminology, 29,* 91–215.

Martinez, R., Stowell, J., & Iwama, J. (2016). The role of immigration: Race/ethnicity and San Diego homicides since 1970. *Journal of Quantitative Criminology, 32,* 471–488.

McClain, C. (1994). *In search of inequality: The Chinese struggle against discrimination in nineteenth-century America.* Berkeley: University of California Press.

McClary, D. (2002). Olmstead, Roy (1886–1966)—King of King County bootleggers. Accessed March 17, 2017 at http://www.historylink.org/File/4015.

McDowall, M., & Wonders, N. (2009). Keeping migrants in their place: Technologies of control and racialized public space in Arizona. *Social Justice, 36,* 54–72.

Miller, H. (2012). Correlates of delinquency and victimization in a sample of Hispanic youth. *International Criminal Justice Review, 22,* 153–170.

Pfaelzer, J. (2007). *Driven out: The forgotten was against Chinese Americans.* New York: Random House.

Portes, A., & Manning, R. (2008). The immigrant enclave: Theory and empirical examples. In D. Grusky (Ed.), *Social stratification: Class, race, and gender in sociological perspective* (pp. 47–68). Boulder, CO: Westview Press.

Provine, D., & Sanchez, G. (2011). Suspecting immigrants: Exploring links between racialized anxieties and expanded police powers in Arizona. *Policing & Society, 21,* 468–479.

Provine, D., Varsanyi, M., Lewis, P., & Decker, S. (2016). *Policing immigrants: Local law enforcement on the front lines.* Chicago, IL: University of Chicago Press.

Rhodan, M. (2017, April 3). Sheriffs may join President Trump's deportation force. *TIME,* 18.

Romero, M. (2006). Racial profiling and immigration law enforcement: Rounding up of usual suspects in the Latino community. *Critical Sociology, 32,* 447–473.

Rosenbloom, R. (2016). Policing sex, policing immigrants: What crimmigration's past can tell us about its present and its future. *California Law Review, 104,* 149–199.

Sampson, R. (2008). Rethinking crime and immigration. *Contexts, 7,* 28–33.

Shaw, C., & McKay, H. (1942). *Juvenile delinquency and urban areas.* Chicago, IL: University of Chicago Press.

Sohoni, D., & Sohoni, T. (2014). Perceptions of immigrant criminality: Crime and social boundaries. *Sociological Quarterly, 55,* 49–71.

Stockwell, A. (1927). Our oldest national problem. *American Journal of Sociology, 32,* 742–755.

Stowell, J., Messner, S., McGeever, K., & Raffalovich, L. (2009). Immigration and the recent violent crime drop in the United States: A pooled, cross-sectional time-series analysis of metropolitan areas. *Criminology, 47,* 889–928.

Stumpf, J. (2006). The crimmigration crisis: Immigrants, crime, and sovereign power. *American University Law Review, 56,* 367–419.

Sung, H., Delgado, S., Peña, D., & Paladino, A. (2016). Surveillance without protection: Policing undocumented migrant workers in an American suburb. *British Journal of Criminology, 56,* 877–897.

Theodore, N. (2011). Policing borders: Unauthorized immigration and the pernicious politics of attrition. *Social Justice, 38,* 90–106.

Timberlake, J., Howell, J., Grau, A., & Williams, R. (2015). Who 'they' are matters: Immigrant stereotypes and assessments of the impact of immigration. *Sociological Quarterly, 56,* 267–299.

Treyger, E., Chalfin, A., & Loeffler, C. (2014). Immigration enforcement, policing, and crime. *Criminology & Public Policy, 13,* 285–322.

Tsai, H. (1986). *The Chinese experience in America.* Bloomington: Indiana University Press.

Vaughan, J. (2006). *Attrition through enforcement: A cost-effective strategy to shrink the illegal population.* Washington, DC: Center for Immigration Studies.

Vaughn, M., Salas-Wright, C., Cooper-Sadlo, S., Maynard, B., & Larson, M. (2015). Are immigrants more likely than native-born Americans to perpetrate intimate partner violence? *Journal of Interpersonal Violence, 30,* 1888–1904.

Walker, S. (1998). *Popular justice: A history of American criminal justice* (2nd ed.). New York: Oxford University Press.

Wilson, J., & Kelling, G. (1982, March). Broken windows: The police and the neighborhood safety. *Atlantic Monthly, 249,* 29–38.

4

The Apparent Immigrants: Latinos' Attitudes Toward the Police

Latino Americans are one of the most visible and fastest growing groups in the U.S. population. In 2001, Latinos exceeded Blacks as the nation's largest minority group, and as of 2015 they comprised roughly 17.6% of the total U.S. population (U.S. Census Bureau, 2016). In the state of California, Latinos have been the largest ethnic group within the state, overtaking non-Hispanic Whites since 2014. It is projected that, by the middle of this century, Latinos will make up at least a quarter of the total U.S. population (Passel & Cohn, 2008). Rapid expansion in the population comes with a growing prominence of Latinos in many spheres of American life, including the field of criminal justice. In 2009, Sonia Sotomayor became the first Latina Supreme Court Justice in American history. Between 2007 and 2013, 60% of the growing number of 13,000 minority police officers across the nation came from the addition of Latino officers (Bekiempis, 2015). Several major American cities, such as Houston, Anaheim, and Santa Ana, have now had Latino police chiefs (Goode, 2016; Huang, 2014).

Despite Latinos' sizable presence and rising social standing within American society, empirical research on Latino Americans' (including Latino immigrants') attitudes toward the police remains sporadic

© The Author(s) 2018
I. Y. Sun and Y. Wu, *Race, Immigration, and Social Control*,
Palgrave Studies in Race, Ethnicity, Indigeneity and Criminal Justice,
https://doi.org/10.1057/978-1-349-95807-8_4

and limited in scope, range and volume. Certainly, not all Latinos are immigrants. Among Latino populations, about 40% are foreign-born, and among these foreign-born Latinos approximately one-fifth (19%) are estimated to be unauthorized (Passel & Cohn, 2009). Latinos' sizable population, coupled with their high percentage of undocumented members, has made them the most obvious immigrant group subject to greater formal social control. Also as a focal concern of the ongoing debates about crime and law enforcement in the media and politics, Latino immigrants' relationships with local police have been challenging, if not outright difficult.

Furthermore, although race/ethnicity has long been recognized as a critical factor in shaping public attitudes toward the police, past research has focused predominately on the experience of Blacks, often in comparison with that of their White counterparts. Such a simplistic Black–White emphasis and contrast is clearly inadequate in accounting for potential racial and ethnic differences in public perceptions of the police. Indeed, given Hispanics' distinct experiences, concerns and expectations of the police as recent voluntary immigrant minorities, their views of the police may not necessarily be in line with that of the Blacks, suggesting the need to give this group of individuals its due attention.

This chapter contains three sections. The first describes the historical and contemporary backgrounds of Latino immigration into the U.S. The second section discusses the constant control exercised by legal authorities on Latinos residing in the country, including research on Latinos' experience with crime and criminal justice. The last section reviews Latinos' perceptions of the police, with comparisons made between Latino and other racial/ethnic groups and attention paid to factors influencing Latinos' opinions on law enforcement agencies including the police.

The Convenient but Disadvantaged Immigrants

The term Latino/as refers to persons of Latin American origin or descent. Although not an entirely homogeneous group and featuring quite diverse subgroups within it, Latinos are often treated as an aggregated ethnic group in official governmental statistics and in academic works. This chapter accordingly reviews their experiences as a whole. Latinos have settled within what is now the U.S. since the mid-sixteenth century. Since the 1960s, Latinos were heavily concentrated in a few states, with Texas, California, Florida, and New Mexico being the principal ones. Recently, however, there is a decline in Latino foreign-born individuals in these traditional receiving states (except for Texas) (Reardon-Anderson, Capps, & Fix, 2002), and meanwhile rapid growth has been taking place in some new receiving states such as North Carolina, Georgia, Nevada, Arkansas, Utah, and Tennessee (Nowak, 2004; Saenz, 2004). Like many other immigrant groups, Latino immigrants are much more geographically dispersed today than ever before in the nation's history.

Latino immigrants as a group have a lower social economic status than some other ethnic groups. Latinos' social disadvantage status is particularly evident in such areas as education and income. In 2002, more than 40% of Latinos aged 25 and older did not graduate from high school, a rate much higher than the 11% of non-Latino Whites (Ramirez & de la Cruz, 2003). Noticeable improvements in Latino high school dropout rates and college enrollment have occurred in the recent decades, however. For example, Latinos' highs school dropout rate has declined drastically from 32% in 2000 to 12% in 2014 among those ages 18–24, and the same age Latino enrollment in two- or four-year colleges has increased from in 22% in 1993 to 35% in 2014 (Krogstad, 2016). Nonetheless, despite these recent gains Latinos still lag behind when it comes to obtaining a bachelor's degree. In 2014, only 15% of Latinos between age 25 and 29 have a four-year college degree or higher compared to 63% of Asians, 41% of non-Hispanic Whites and 22% of Blacks of the same age group (Krogstad, 2016). Due partly to their relatively low levels of education, Latinos are more likely than non-White Hispanics to work in service occupations or as operators and laborers, earn less, and live in poverty (Ramirez & de la Cruz, 2003). Similar to the effect of immigration status, such demographic characteristics as education and income often subject Latinos to more formal social control, including that from the law enforcement and corrections sectors of society.

For many immigrants, including Latinos, life in a foreign country is often stressful. Caplan (2007) delineated three primary types of stressors present among Latino immigrants: *instrumental/environmental, social/ interpersonal,* and *societal.* The term instrumental/environmental stressors refers to challenges attached to obtaining the goods and services needed for one's daily life, such as employment, access to health care, and language training. For example, to find work by meeting potential employers in public spaces, undocumented Latino labor workers utilize such tactics as avoiding the police and displaying great deference to local non-Hispanic White residents while adroitly using all the leverage possible to negotiate better compensation (Cleaveland & Pierson, 2009). Latino day laborers are typically more likely to experience wage theft by both unscrupulous employers and by criminal middle men than other groups. These parties generally believe that these undocumented workers are unlikely to report their victimization to the police due to their undocumented status (Fussell, 2011).

Social and interpersonal stressors involve the challenges associated with establishing sources of family and social support, changing gender roles and family responsibilities and experiencing intergenerational conflicts. These challenges have proven to be difficult for many immigrant families regardless of their racial or ethnic backgrounds (Alvarez-Rivera, Nobles, & Lersch, 2014). Research carried out among Latinos in a number of *barrios* (areas of concentrated Latino settlement with many persons and family living at subsistence levels) has shown that among Latino adolescents growing up in families with unauthorized immigrant members, a lack of adequate parental involvement and support is often to be found. These circumstances of childhood experience are associated with great stress, raising the likelihood of lifetime marijuana and cigarette use (Roblyer, Grzywacz, Cervantes, & Merten, 2016).

Societal stressors reflect discrimination and difficulties attached to an undocumented status, principally fear of deportation. Arbona and colleagues (2010) found in their work that the fear of deportation is the strongest predictor of acculturative stress among both documented and undocumented Latino immigrants. Even when immigration legal status (i.e., documented versus undocumented) and immigration-related challenges had been controlled in their analysis, fear of deportation was still significantly associated with stress and anxiety. Such fear, unfortunately, discourages immigrants, undocumented particularly, from seeking help for employment, health, and language training, further increasing the stress that they already experience in life as a foreign-born individual (Rodriguez & Hagan, 2004; Sullivan & Rehm, 2005).

Unequally Targeted by Law Enforcement

Latino concerns about deportation, which has disproportionately targeted Latino working class men (Golash-Boza & Hondagneu-Sotelo, 2013), have been high since the passage of the 1996 immigration and welfare reform laws (Hagan & Rodriguez, 2002). One study examining generational differences among Latino immigrants found that legal consciousness constituted a primary source of fear among undocumented first-generation immigrants and was heavily infused with stigma among the 1.5 generation counterparts as well (Abrego, 2011). During the past two decades, fear, stigma, and worries regarding immigration enforcement have indeed continued to rise, corresponding to both a national and a local trend of using various types of laws to criminalize undocumented immigrants. For example, the passage of Hazelton, Pennsylvania's Illegal Immigrant Relief Act in 2006 was chiefly a result of moral panic among non-Hispanic White residents. The degradation of Latino immigrants was employed by local officials to ensure the continuance of non-Hispanic White social supremacy and reaffirm the racial and ethnic social order in the community (Longazel, 2012).

As mentioned in Chapter 3, the "Chandler roundup" is an example of ethnic profiling targeted specifically at Latino immigrants. Similarly, Arizona's SB 1070 enacted into law in 2011 requires state and local law enforcement to verify a person's citizenship status whenever they have reasonable suspicion that the person is undocumented. This is another example of the broadest, strictest, and most controversial anti-immigration measures (Fisher, Deason, Borgida, & Oyamot, 2011) having a particularly profound impact on the nation's Latino population.

Although most police agencies in the country have reported that they do not directly enforce immigration laws (Lewis, Provine,

Varsanyi, & Decker, 2012), Immigration and Customs Enforcement (ICE) has often identified, detained, and removed noncitizens from the country through inspection of state and local jails (Eagly, 2013; Pedroza, 2013). Diaz (2011) has argued that contemporary U.S. immigration policies and enforcement practices have created an Immigration Industrial Complex (IIC). Similar to the Prison Industrial Complex, the IIC is an industry supported by Congressional powers, based on immigrant detainees, and used to expunge Latino immigrants from the U.S. to protect the White hegemonic order. A before-and-after study of extended local police power in immigration enforcement in Costa Mesa, California confirmed that aggressive immigration enforcement by local police has led to more police stops of fully documented and legal Latino residents. Persons experiencing this treatment (personally and vicariously) expressed less favorable attitudes toward the police and were less likely to report crime to the police (Vidales, Day, & Powe, 2009).

Aggressive law enforcement against Latino immigrants has its roots in racial and ethnic prejudice. Despite some positive perceptions (e.g., strong family and values of salvation), Latinos are often associated with some negative stereotypes viewing them as lazy, less intelligent, poorly educated and more violent and rebellious (Fairchild & Cozens, 1981; Jackson et al., 1996). They also suffer negative images as persons not legally residing in the nation and being more prone to crime. These misconceptions, combined with the reality that newer arrivals are often economically disadvantaged and socially isolated, have fostered an impression that Latinos pose a problem and a danger to the U.S. society (Fix & Passel, 2001).

Complicating matters further, terms such as "criminal aliens" and other criminalizing rhetoric that some politicians use mislead the public to believe that undocumented immigrants are in high proportion criminals and threats to American communities. Even the current president, Donald Trump, made extremely controversial rants during his election campaign against Mexican migrants as drug smugglers, criminals and rapists, and repeatedly promised to build a border wall to keep these undesirable criminal immigrants out. This hostility, at least insensitivity, from the highest leader of the country toward Latino immigrants has reflected a culture of fear in this nation toward "others,"

Latinos included. The inflaming of ethnic animosity has undoubtedly instilled great fear and anxiety among people of Latino descent. A recent survey of Latino adults conducted by the Pew Research Center before Trump's inauguration indicated a rising percentage of Latinos believing that the situation of U.S. Latinos is worsening. The results of that survey revealed that as many as half of the Latino respondents were worried about the deportation of someone they know (Pew Research Center, 2017). Research also found that, not surprisingly, U.S.-born Mexican Americans expressed greater support for the criminalization of immigration compared to foreign-born Mexican Americans and non-citizen Mexicans (Barboza, Dominguez, Siller, & Montalva, 2017). Similarly, public perceptions of Latino political and economic threats were closely linked to survey respondents' support for aggressive policing tactics against suspects (Pickett, 2016).

The derogatory stereotyping of Latino immigrants as being prone to crime is not supported by any concrete research evidence. Actually, immigrants as a whole are far less likely to commit crimes than their native-born counterparts. In an official statement issued by the American Society of Criminology Executive Board concerning the Trump Administration's policies relevant to crime and justice in 2017, leading criminological scholars, based on a century's worth of findings on immigration and crime in the U.S., concluded that immigrants do not commit the majority of crime in the nation as has been claimed (Lynch et al., 2017). To the contrary, immigrant concentration has been shown to lower crime at the neighborhood and city levels alike. This phenomenon is commonly known as the revitalization thesis, and in most cases immigration is a protective factor against crime at the individual level as well (Lynch et al., 2017). Looking specifically at the crime of homicide in El Paso, Texas, a predominately Latino city, researchers found that social disorganization variables, such as concentrated disadvantage and residential mobility, were significantly related to total homicide, but percent immigrant and percent black were not linked to any homicide measures (Emerick, Curry, Collins, & Rodriguez, 2014).

Specifically regarding Latino immigrants, Hagan and Palloni (1999) explained that government reports of growing numbers of Latino immigrants in U.S. prisons do not mean that Latino immigrants are more inclined to commit crime. In fact, after taking two important factors into account, crime involvement by Latino immigrants is less than that of non-Hispanic Whites. The first factor is that Latino immigrants are disproportionately young males who, regardless of citizenship and ethnicity, are at greater risk of criminal involvement. The second factor is that Latino immigrants are more vulnerable to restrictive treatment and process outcomes during the criminal justice process, especially at pre-trial stages. When these two factors are taken into consideration the level of involvement of Latino immigrants in crime is actually lower than that of citizens. Interestingly, research done in this area also indicates that a significant connection exists between acculturation and crime among Latino immigrants, even controlling for factors such as race, sex, socioeconomic status, and the presence of drugs (Alvarez-Rivera et al., 2014).

Unfortunately, despite accounting for a smaller proportion of crime, Latino immigrants are at a higher risk of being detained, arrested and sentenced than non-immigrants (Hagan & Palloni, 1999). Relative to their proportion in the U.S. population, people of Latino descent are overrepresented in criminal justice official statistics too (Aguirre & Baker, 2000). Based on sentencing data from Pennsylvania, Steffensmeier and Demuth (2001) found that Latino defendants, compared to non-Hispanic Whites and Blacks, are at the highest risk to receive the harshest penalty across different types of charges and sentencing decisions. Regrettably, little data are available for analysis regarding the situation for foreign-born Latinos in specific with regard to their status in the criminal justice process and prosecutorial and judicial decision-making outcomes.

Latino Perceptions of the Police

It is recognized that many of the reasons that explain why Latino immigrant communities may have a strained relationship with local police are similar to those found in other minority communities in the U.S., including selective law enforcement, often brutal acts of violence, violations of civil and political rights, and other coercive measures (Ammar, Orloff, Dutton, & Aguilar-Hass, 2005; Perilla, 1999). The above-mentioned disjunction between levels of criminality and criminalization can also undermine Latino immigrants' perceptions of the fairness of the police (Cavanagh & Cauffman, 2015a) and strengthen their suspicions of police racial profiling (Romero, 2006).

One additional noteworthy component in the difficult relationship between the police and Latinos includes police officers' threats of deportation and reporting of non-citizen victims and witnesses to federal authorities (Ammar et al., 2005; Orloff, Dutton, Aguilar-Hass, & Ammar, 2003). Based on two years of fieldwork with the Metropolitan Nashville Police Department, Armenta (2015) found that the local police faced a major dilemma in this era of heightened immigration control. On one hand, the department has an official community policing program that aims to build trust and promote communication with Latino immigrant residents. On the other hand, patrol officers undermine these well-meaning goals and objectives by citing and arresting many Latino residents who lack a state-issued ID. Thus, despite some genuine hope to improve police-Latino community relations, line officers have often performed tightened social control and urban discipline on immigrants through their discretionary decision-making, ultimately weakening the potential benefits of community policing efforts (Armenta, 2015).

Tightened immigrant enforcement tactics exacerbate immigrants' anxiety about any type of police contacts (Nguyen & Gill, 2016; Stuesse & Coleman, 2014). Indeed, immigrants as a group tend to go out of their way to avoid contacts with the police to a far greater degree than native-born Americans (Davis & Hendricks, 2007). Davis and Miller (2002) reported that residents of the predominantly immigrant communities they studied were less likely to be aware of community policing programs and less likely to participate in those efforts than residents of longer-established ethnic communities. Davis and Henderson (2003) also demonstrated that members of well-established communities were more willing to report crimes to the police than members of largely recently arrived immigrant communities. Immigrant Latina women were found to severely underreport their victimization of intimate partner violence, and assessment of police response when the crime was reported was portrayed as reflecting a lack of cultural sensitivity (Ammar et al., 2005). Another study carried out in this area of police interactions found that Latino immigrants reported roughly one-third of their violent victimization experiences, and incidents involving serious injury, multiple victims, and perceptions of discrimination were more likely to be reported to the police (Hautala, Dombrowski, & Marcus, 2015). In Los Angeles, foreign-born Latinos were less inclined than U.S.-born non-Hispanic Whites and African Americans to report unfair treatment by the police (Bjornstrom, 2015). Latinos' reluctance to report victimization and unfair treatment experienced unfortunately further compromises police effectiveness and fairness in controlling public safety threats and preventing crime in immigrant neighborhoods.

While growing in frequency, empirical research on Latino perceptions of the police remains rather limited and largely inconclusive. For instance, two early studies showed that Latinos have less favorable views of the police than the general public (Carter, 1985; Mirande, 1981). Some recent studies, in contrast, have suggested that Latino attitudes are in the middle ground between those of non-Hispanic Whites and Blacks (Buckler & Unnever, 2008; Lai & Zhao, 2010; Miller & Davis, 2008; Ong & Jenks, 2004; Schuck & Rosenbaum, 2005; Skogan, 2006; Skogan, Steiner, DuBois, Gudeel, & Fagan, 2002; Weitzer, 2002). Compared to non-Hispanic Whites, Latinos are more likely to view the police as using excessive force (Cheurprakobkit & Bartsch, 1999; Skogan, 2005), and as being unfair, impolite, and unhelpful (Skogan, 2005). Other studies have suggested that Latinos do not necessarily always occupy an in-between position in the racial hierarchy of public assessments of the police. One study, for example, specifically reported that although Latinos are found to be more critical than non-Hispanic Whites and less critical than Blacks in viewing police hassling and racial profiling, they hold largely similar opinions to those of non-Hispanic Whites in regard to police bias and problem solving (Wu, 2014). Still other studies (e.g., Correia, 2010) indicated that Latino immigrants hold the police in higher regard than non-immigrants, especially in such evaluative areas as police accountability and misconduct (Schuck, Rosenbaum, & Hawkins, 2008; Weitzer & Tuch, 2006).

In the majority-minority city of San Antonio, Texas, for example, Latinos expressed higher degrees of satisfaction with the police than their non-Hispanic White counterparts (McCluskey, McCluskey, & Enriquez, 2008). Latino immigrants also rendered more favorable evaluations of the police than their non-immigrant counterparts (Correia, 2010). Among Latino immigrants, those who arrived at the U.S. through illegal channels were found to be significantly more likely to express unfavorable attitudes toward the police than those who relocated through legal channels (Roles, Moak, & Bensel, 2016).

These diverse findings highlight the complexity of comparative ratings of the police between Latino and other racial/ethnic groups, and within Latino groups. Research that classifies Latinos as either Whites/majorities or non-Whites/minorities is clearly inadequate in assessing their attitudes toward the police. So is research that fails to distinguish between US-born and foreign-born individuals of Latino descent, making it impossible to assess Latino foreign-borns' unique experiences and perceptions, separate from the rest of the U.S. Latino population.

Similar to findings in the broad literature on the general public (see Brown & Benedict, 2002), Latino personal demographics are only weakly related to their opinions on the police. When the impact is identified, it tends to be inconsistent, and at times even contradictory. Using age as an example, two studies found a non-significant link between age and Latino evaluations of the police (Messing, Becerra, Ward-Lasher, & Androff, 2015; Ong & Jenks, 2004). A third study, however, demonstrated a positive connection between age and Latino satisfaction with the police (McCluskey et al., 2008), and still another fourth study reported a negative association between age and Latino non-immigrant perceptions of the police—but a non-significant relationship of age and Latino immigrant perceptions of the police (Correia, 2010).

Among Latino foreign-born individuals, perhaps one of the most prominent obstacles during police-immigrant contacts is that of language (Davies & Fagan, 2012). Inability to communicate effectively often constitutes a source of frustration for both immigrants and police officers. As noted by Skogan (2005), communication is key to increasing the quality of treatment during contact with the police, which subsequently increases satisfaction with the police. In his study, Skogan (2005) found that speaking Spanish was not a significant direct predictor of satisfaction with the police, but it was mediated by the quality of treatment the individual received. The same study also found that those who spoke Spanish tended to view police-initiated encounters more critically than Caucasians taken as a comparison group.

Police quality of treatment may be directly affected by the quality of communication between officers and Latino immigrants. Failure to effectively communicate with immigrants by the police can increase the likelihood of cultural misunderstandings, and such a failure in communication has the potential to aggravate Latino fear of and mistrust in the police (Lewis & Ramakrishnan, 2007; Waslin, 2007). These negative emotions and perceptions can further damage police-immigrant interactions (Culver, 2004). Assessing the impact of community policing efforts on Latino residents, Torres and Vogel (2001) found that bilingual officers allowed for more effective communication and may have been responsible for the positive changes found in Latino perceptions over the course of their study. Overall, evidence exists to suggest benefits pertain to reducing the linguistic barrier between the police and Latino immigrants in the form of promoting mutually respectful relationships (Davis & Erez, 1998; Erez & Globokar, 2007; Lewis & Ramakrishnan, 2007; Menjivar & Bejarano, 2004).

Besides language proficiency, cultural differences may also affect Latino immigrants' attitudes toward the police. Latino culture, for example, places great value on familial support and obligations, traditional gender roles, and personal relationships (Ammar et al., 2005; Erez & Globokar, 2007; Lewis & Ramakrishnan, 2007; Menjivar & Bejarano, 2004). A lack of understanding of these cultural traits may lead to officers' culturally inappropriate responses, creating misunderstanding between the police and community residents and amplifying chances of negative interactions and the provision of poor services (Ammar et al., 2005; Menjivar & Bejarano, 2004).

Influence from one's country of origin goes beyond language and cultural values. Immigrants' prior experience with and perceptions of their home country legal authorities may impede their positive interaction with the U.S. police as well. Menjivar and Bejarano (2004) found that Latino immigrants tend to view their current experiences in the U.S.

in comparison to their experiences with political and legal officials in their home country. They argue that immigrants tend to perceive criminal justice experiences through "bifocal lenses," those pertaining to their home country and those pertaining to their host country in various aspects of political, economic, and social life (Menjivar & Bejarano, 2004). Negative experiences with home country police thus may hinder Latino immigrants' positive expectations and interactions with the U.S. police.

Immigrant generational status can affect their attitudes toward the police. Based on a Seattle sample with its immigrant respondents being primarily either a Latino or Asian, Davis and Hendricks (2007) found that immigrants in Seattle had a more positive view of the police than non-immigrants. In particular, immigrants had a greater confidence in police integrity and fairness—they were significantly less likely to believe that officers would stop people without a good reason, engage in racial profiling, and verbally or physically abuse citizens. Seattle immigrants also gave higher ratings to police effectiveness. Another study conducted with Latino immigrants in Reno, Nevada, echoed these findings by showing that immigrants had more favorable views of the police than non-immigrants in various evaluative areas such as fairness, honesty, and provision of equal treatment (Correia, 2010). Based on data from Queens, NY, Davis and Mateu-Gelabert (2000) reported that respondents from ethnic communities with large proportions of recent immigrants reported lower evaluations of the police than ethnic communities with greater proportions of US-born residents or residents with longer residence in the country. It is unclear, however, in this study if foreign-born immigrants were more critical of the police than their native-born counterparts as we cannot make inferences about the nature of individuals from patterns of the groups.

Immigration (legal) status also matters in Latino immigrant attitudes toward the police. Cavanagh and Cauffman (2015b) found that youth whose mothers were undocumented held more negative perceptions of the police than youth whose mothers were documented. In addition, undocumented youth themselves were also more likely to have negative perceptions of the police compared to their documented counterparts. The study youths, however, did not perceive judges differently based on mother's documentation status. Therefore, the police suffer more from deportation policies despite it being the case that deportation is ultimately up to judges to decide. Cavanagh and Cauffman (2015b) explained that this is probably because the police are the most visible "face" of the law. As gatekeepers of the criminal justice process, the police tend to be seen as the principal agitator of a deportation. Indeed, Goff and colleagues (2013) have shown that policies that cast the police as the face of immigration enforcement reduce views of the police as legitimate.

Summary

Latinos have been a principal minority group in the country's long history of immigration, and they continue to occupy the central stage in public debates about and sentiment toward immigration, immigration policy and the enforcement of immigration law. Given Latinos' high proportions among both U.S.-born residents/legal immigrants and undocumented immigrants, they have become the most convenient targets of immigration control and enforcement. Their relatively disadvantaged social status in terms of education, occupations, and income has further deepened their vulnerability in facing discrimination and biased enforcement of state-level criminal statutes and federal immigration policies and regulations.

Historical racial and ethnic prejudice constitutes the fundamental underlying cause of aggressive law enforcement against Latino immigrants. There is an impression among many Americans that Latino immigrants pose a public health and safety problem and a danger to U.S. society, and a **criminal alien** image attached to Latino immigrants is often deliberately spread by some politicians to maintain non-Hispanic White supremacy over Latinos and justify racialized law enforcement against immigrants.

Despite these vulnerabilities, Latinos have yet to receive proportionate attention in the existing research literature, with empirical research on Latino perceptions of the police remaining exceedingly limited and inconclusive in its overall findings. Comparative analyses of public opinion on the police between Latino and other racial/ethnic groups, and among Latino groups, also have yielded inconsistent results due chiefly to differences in samples studied and variation in measurements taken. Immigrant-specific factors, such as language proficiency, country of origin, and immigration status, appear to have a stronger correlation than individual demographic characteristics with Latinos' evaluations of the police.

References

Abrego, L. (2011). Legal consciousness of undocumented Latinos: Fear and stigma as barriers to claims-making for first- and 1.5-generation immigrants. *Law & Society Review, 45,* 337–369.

Aguirre, A., Jr., & Baker, D. (2000). Latinos and the United States criminal justice system: Introduction. *Criminal Justice Studies, 13,* 3–6.

Alvarez-Rivera, L., Nobles, M., & Lersch, K. (2014). Latino immigrant acculturation and crime. *American Journal of Criminal Justice, 39,* 315–330.

Ammar, N., Orloff, L., Dutton, M., & Aguilar-Hass, G. (2005). Calls to police and police response: A case study from the Latina immigrant women in the U.S. *Journal of International Police Science and Management, 7,* 230–244.

Arbona, C., Olvera, N., Rodriguez, N., Hagan, J., Linares, A., & Wiesner, M. (2010). Acculturative stress among documented and undocumented Latino immigrants in the United States. *Hispanic Journal of Behavioral Sciences, 32,* 362–384.

Armenta, A. (2015). Between public service and social control: Policing dilemmas in the era of immigration enforcement. *Social Problems, 63,* 111–126.

Barboza, G., Dominguez, S., Siller, L., & Montalva, M. (2017). Citizenship, fear and support for the criminalization of immigration: Contextualizing Mexican Americans' attitudes about the role of law enforcement. *Policing: An International Journal of Police Strategies & Management, 40,* 197–213.

Bekiempis, V. (2015). The new racial makeup of U.S. police departments. *Newsweek.* Accessed May 1, 2017 at http://www.newsweek.com/racial-makeup-police-departments-331130.

Bjornstrom, E. (2015). Race-ethnicity, nativity, neighborhood context and reported unfair treatment by police. *Ethnic and Racial Studies, 38,* 2019–2036.

Brown, B., & Benedict, W. (2002). Perceptions of the police: Past findings, methodological issues, conceptual issues and policy implications. *Policing: An International Journal of Police Strategies & Management, 25,* 543–580.

Buckler, K., & Unnever, J. (2008). Racial and ethnic perceptions of injustice: Testing the core hypotheses of comparative conflict theory. *Journal of Criminal Justice, 36,* 270–278.

Caplan, S. (2007). Latinos, acculturation, and acculturative stress: A dimensional concept analysis. *Policy, Politics, and Nursing Practice, 8,* 93–106.

Carter, D. (1985). Hispanic perception of police performance: An empirical assessment. *Journal of Criminal Justice, 13,* 487–500.

Cavanagh, C., & Cauffman, E. (2015a). The land of the free: Undocumented families in the juvenile justice system. *Law and Human Behavior, 39,* 152–161.

Cavanagh, C., & Cauffman, E. (2015b). Viewing law and order: Mothers' and sons' justice system legitimacy attitudes and juvenile recidivism. *Psychology, Public Policy, and Law, 21,* 432–441.

Cheurprakobkit, S., & Bartsch, R. (1999). Police work and the police profession: Assessing attitudes of city officials, Spanish-speaking Hispanics, and their English-speaking counterparts. *Journal of Criminal Justice, 27,* 87–100.

Cleaveland, C., & Pierson, L. (2009). Parking lots and police: Undocumented Latinos' tactics for finding day labor jobs. *Ethnography, 10,* 515–533.

Correia, M. (2010). Determinants of attitudes toward the police of Latino immigrants and non-immigrants. *Journal of Criminal Justice, 38,* 99–107.

Culver, L. (2004). The impact of new immigration patterns on the provision of police services in Midwestern communities. *Journal of Criminal Justice, 32,* 329–344.

Davies, G., & Fagan, J. (2012). Crime and enforcement in immigrant neighborhoods: Evidence from New York City. *The Annals of the American Academy of Political and Social Science, 641,* 99–124.

Davis, R., & Erez, E. (1998). *Immigrant populations as victims: Toward a multicultural criminal justice system* (NCJ 167571). Washington, DC: U.S. Department of Justice.

Davis, R., & Henderson, N. (2003). Willingness to report crimes: The role of ethnic group membership and community efficacy. *NCCD News, 49,* 564–580.

Davis, R., & Hendricks, N. (2007). Immigrants and law enforcement: A comparison of native-born and foreign-born Americans' opinions of the police. *International Review of Victimology, 14,* 81–94.

Davis, R., & Mateu-Gelabert, P. (2000, July). Effective police management affects citizen perceptions. *National Institute of Justice Journal, (244)*, 24–25.

Davis, R., & Miller, J. (2002). Immigration and integration: Perceptions of community policing among members of six ethnic communities in central Queens, New York City. *International Review of Victimology, 9,* 93–111.

Diaz, J. (2011). Immigration policy, criminalization and the growth of the immigration industrial complex: Restriction, expulsion, and eradication of the undocumented in the US. *Western Criminology Review, 12,* 35–54.

Eagly, I. (2013). Criminal justice for noncitizens: An analysis of variation in local enforcement. *New York University Law Review, 88,* 1126–1223.

Emerick, N., Curry, T., Collins, T., & Rodriguez, S. (2014). Homicide and social disorganization on the border: Implications for Latino and immigrant populations. *Social Science Quarterly, 95,* 360–379.

Erez, E., & Globokar, J. (2007). Immigrant women, domestic violence, and community policing. *Law Enforcement Executive Forum, 7,* 1–14.

Fairchild, H., & Cozens, J. (1981). Chicano, Hispanic, or Mexican American: What's in a name? *Hispanic Journal of Behavioral Sciences, 3,* 191–198.

Fisher, E., Deason, G., Borgida, E., & Oyamot, C. (2011). A model of authoritarianism, social norms, and personal values: Implications for Arizona law enforcement and immigration policy. *Analyses of Social Issues and Public Policy, 11,* 285–299.

Fix, M., & Passel, J. (2001). *U.S. immigration at the beginning of the 21st century.* Testimony before the Subcommittee on Immigration and Claims Hearing on the US Population and Immigration, Committee on the Judiciary, U.S. House of Representatives, August 2, 2001.

Fussell, E. (2011). The deportation threat dynamic and victimization of Latino migrants: Wage theft and robbery. *The Sociological Quarterly, 52,* 593–615.

Golash-Boza, T., & Hondagneu-Sotelo, P. (2013). Latino immigrant men and the deportation crisis: A gendered racial removal program. *Latino Studies, 11,* 271–292.

Goff, P., Epstein, L., & Reddy, K. (2013). Crossing the line of legitimacy: The impact of cross-deputization policy on crime reporting. *Psychology, Public Policy, and Law, 19,* 250–258.

Goode, J. (2016). *Houston welcomes first Latino police chief, Art Acevedo.* Accessed July 5, 2017 at http://stylemagazine.com/news/2016/dec/02/houston-welcomes-first-latino-police-chief-art-ace/.

Hagan, J., & Palloni, A. (1999). Sociological criminology and the mythology of Hispanic immigration and crime. *Social Problems, 46,* 617–632.

Hagan, J., & Rodriguez, N. (2002). Resurrecting exclusion: The effects of 1996 immigration reform on families and communities in Texas, Mexico and El Salvador. In M. Suarez-Orozco & M. Paez (Eds.), *Latinos: Remaking America* (pp. 190–201). Los Angeles, CA: University of California Press.

Hautala, D., Dombrowski, K., & Marcus, A. (2015). Predictors of police reporting among Hispanic immigrant victims of violence. *Race and Justice, 5,* 235–258.

Huang, J. (2014). *In a first for Orange County, Latinos lead two largest police departments.* Accessed July 1, 2017 at http://www.scpr.org/blogs/multiamerican/2014/05/08/16582/orange-county-latinos-police-quezada-rojas/.

Jackson, L., Hodge, C., Gerard, D., Ingram, J., Ervin, K., & Sheppard, L. (1996). Cognition, affect, and behavior in the prediction of group attitudes. *Personality and Social Psychology Bulletin, 22,* 306–316.

Krogstad, J. (2016). *5 facts about Latinos and education.* Pew Research Center. Accessed April 17, 2017 at http://www.pewresearch.org/fact-tank/2016/07/28/5-facts-about-latinos-and-education/.

Lai, Y., & Zhao, J. (2010). The impact of race/ethnicity, neighborhood context, and police/citizen interaction on residents' attitudes toward the police. *Journal of Criminal Justice, 38,* 685–692.

Lewis, P., Provine, D., Varsanyi, M., & Decker, S. (2012). Why do (some) city police departments enforce federal immigration law? Political, demographic, and organizational influences on local choices. *Journal of Public Administration Research and Theory, 23,* 1–25.

Lewis, P., & Ramakrishnan, S. (2007). Police practices in immigrant-destination cities: Political control or bureaucratic professionalism? *Urban Affairs Review, 42,* 874–900.

Longazel, J. (2012). Moral panic as racial degradation ceremony: Racial stratification and the local-level backlash against Latino/a immigrants. *Punishment and Society, 15,* 96–119.

Lynch, J., et al. (2017). *Statement of the American Society of Criminology Executive Board concerning the Trump administration's policies relevant to crime and justice.* Accessed June 18, 2017 at https://www.asc41.com/policies/ASC_Executive_Board_Statement_on_Trump_Administration_Crime_and_Justice_Policies.pdf.

McCluskey, J., McCluskey, C., & Enriquez, R. (2008). A comparison of Latino and White citizen satisfaction with police. *Journal of Criminal Justice, 36,* 471–477.

Menjivar, C., & Bejarano, C. (2004). Latino immigrants' perceptions of crime and police authorities in the United States: A case study from the Phoenix metropolitan area. *Ethnic and Racial Studies, 27,* 120–148.

Messing, J., Becerra, D., Ward-Lasher, A., & Androff, D. (2015). Latinas' perceptions of law enforcement: Fear of deportation, crime reporting, and trust in the system. *Journal of Women and Social Work, 30,* 328–340.

Miller, J., & Davis, R. C. (2008). Unpacking public attitudes to the police: Contrasting perceptions of misconduct with traditional measures of satisfaction. *International Journal of Police Science and Management, 10,* 9–22.

Mirande, A. (1981). The Chicano and the law: An analysis of community-police conflict in an urban Barrio. *The Pacific Sociological Review, 24,* 65–86.

Nguyen, M., & Gill, H. (2016). Interior immigration enforcement: The impacts of expanding local law enforcement authority. *Urban Studies, 53,* 302–323.

Nowak, M. (2004). *Immigration and U.S. population growth: An environmental perspective.* Negative Population Growth, Special Report. Accessed February 10, 2005 at http://www.npg.org/specialreports/imm&uspopgrowth.htm.

Ong, M., & Jenks, D. (2004). Hispanic perceptions of community policing. *Journal of Ethnicity in Criminal Justice, 2,* 53–66.

Orloff, L., Dutton, M., Aguilar-Hass, G., & Ammar, N. (2003). Battered immigrant women's willingness to call for help and police response. *UCLA Women's Law Journal, 13,* 43–100.

Passel, J., & Cohn, D. (2008). *U.S. population projections: 2005–2025.* Pew Research Center Hispanic Trends. Accessed April 11, 2017 at http://www.pewhispanic.org/2008/02/11/us-population-projections-2005-2050/.

Passel, J., & Cohn, D. (2009). *A portrait of unauthorized immigrants in the United States.* Washington, DC: The Pew Hispanic Center.

Pedroza, J. (2013). Removal roulette: Secure communities and immigration enforcement in the United States (2008–2012). In D. Brotherton, D. Stageman, & S. Leyro (Eds.), *Outside justice* (pp. 45–68). New York: Springer.

Perilla, J. (1999). Domestic violence as a human rights issue: The case of immigrant Latinos. *Hispanic Journal of Behavioral Sciences, 21,* 107–133.

Pew Research Center. (2017). *Latinos and the new Trump administration.* Accessed July 1, 2017 at http://www.pewhispanic.org/2017/02/23/latinos-and-the-new-trump-administration/.

Pickett, J. (2016). On the social foundation for *crimmigration*: Latino threat and support for expanded police powers. *Journal of Quantitative Criminology, 32,* 103–132.

Ramirez, R., & de la Cruz, P. (2003). *The Hispanic population in the United States: March 2002.* Accessed April 17, 2017 at https://www.census.gov/prod/2003pubs/p20-545.pdf.

Reardon-Anderson, J., Capps, R., & Fix, M. (2002). *The health and wellbeing of children in immigrant families: Assessing the new Federalism Policy Brief B-52*. Washington, DC: The Urban Institute.

Roblyer, M., Grzywacz, J., Cervantes, R., & Merten, M. (2016). Stress and alcohol, cigarette, and marijuana use among Latino adolescents in families with undocumented immigrants. *Journal of Child and Family Studies, 25*, 475–487.

Rodriguez, N., & Hagan, J. (2004). Fractured families and communities: Effects of immigration reform in Texas, Mexico, and El Salvador. *Latino Studies, 2*, 328–351.

Roles, R., Moak, S., & Bensel, T. (2016). Perceptions of police among Hispanic immigrants of Mexican origin in the southeast United States. *American Journal of Criminal Justice, 41*, 202–219.

Romero, M. (2006). Racial profiling and immigration law enforcement: Rounding up of usual suspects in the Latino community. *Critical Sociology, 32*, 447–473.

Saenz, R. (2004). *Latinos and the changing face of America at the turn of the century*. Russell Sage Foundation, Population Reference Bureau. Accessed November 7, 2017 at http://www.prb.org/Publications/Articles/2004/LatinosandtheChangingFaceofAmerica.aspx.

Schuck, A., & Rosenbaum, D. (2005). Global and neighborhood attitudes toward the police: Differentiation by race, ethnicity, and type of contact. *Journal of Quantitative Criminology, 21*, 391–418.

Schuck, A., Rosenbaum, D., & Hawkins, D. (2008). The influence of race/ethnicity, social class, and neighborhood context on residents: Attitudes toward the police. *Police Quarterly, 11*, 496–519.

Skogan, W. (2005). Citizen satisfaction with police encounters. *Police Quarterly, 8*, 298–321.

Skogan, W. (2006). Community policing and the new immigrants: Latinos in Chicago. In M. King (Ed.), *Justice and safety in America's immigrant communities* (pp. 43–64). Princeton, NJ: Policy Research Institute for the Region, Princeton University.

Skogan, W., Steiner, L., DuBois, J., Gudeel, E., & Fagan, A. (2002). *Community policing and "the new immigrants": Latinos in Chicago*. Evanston, IL: Institute for Police Research, Northwestern University.

Steffensmeier, D., & Demuth, S. (2001). Ethnicity and judges' sentencing decisions: Hispanic-Black-White comparisons. *Criminology, 39*, 145–178.

Stuesse, A., & Coleman, M. (2014). Automobility, immobility, altermobility: Surviving and resisting the intensification of immigrant policing. *City & Society, 26*, 51–72.

Sullivan, M., & Rehm, R. (2005). Mental health of undocumented Mexican immigrants: A review of the literature. *Advances in Nursing Sciences, 28,* 240–251.

Torres, S., & Vogel, R. (2001). Pre- and post-test differences between Vietnamese and Latino residents involved in a community policing experiment: Reducing fear of crime and improving attitudes towards the police. *Policing: An International Journal of Police Strategies & Management, 24,* 40–55.

U.S. Census Bureau. (2016). *FFF: Hispanic Heritage Month.* Accessed May 10, 2017 at https://www.census.gov/newsroom/facts-for-features/2016/cb16-ff16.html.

Vidales, G., Day, K., & Powe, M. (2009). Police and immigration enforcement: Impacts on Latino(a) residents' perceptions of police. *Policing: An International Journal of Police Strategies and Management, 32,* 631–653.

Waslin, M. (2007). Immigration enforcement by local and state police: The impact on Latinos. *Law Enforcement Executive Forum, 7,* 15–28.

Weitzer, R. (2002). Incidents of police misconduct and public opinion. *Journal of Criminal Justice, 30,* 397–408.

Weitzer, R., & Tuch, S. (2006). *Race and policing in America: Conflict and reform.* New York: Cambridge University Press.

Wu, Y. (2014). Race/ethnicity and perceptions of the police: A comparison of White, Black, Asian and Hispanic Americans. *Policing and Society, 24,* 135–157.

5

Model Minorities and Forever Foreigners: Chinese Americans' Attitudes Toward the Police

The Asian population in the U.S. has grown rapidly over the past few decades, increasing from 1.5 million in 1970 to 17.3 million by 2010. Between 2000 and 2015, the U.S. Asian population grew 72% from 11.9 million to 20.4 million, making them the fastest growth rate of any major racial or ethnic group (Lopez, Ruiz, & Patten, 2017). It is expected that Asians will become the largest immigrant group in the country, surpassing Latinos in 2055 (Lopez et al., 2017). Although race remains a prominent characteristic in policing, only very limited research has examined the law enforcement-related experiences and opinions of Asian Americans. As a racial minority group, Asian Americans may occupy a social position similar to that of other minority groups, and accordingly display less positive views regarding the police than their White counterparts. Alternatively, due to different immigration histories, levels of racial consciousness, and imposed stereotypes—among other factors—Asian Americans may have distinct experiences with and perceptions of the police from those of other minority groups. Further, since most Asian Americans at this point are foreign-born (Grieco, 2010), race and immigrant status may intersect with one another, complicating Asian Americans' attitudes

© The Author(s) 2018
I. Y. Sun and Y. Wu, *Race, Immigration, and Social Control,*
Palgrave Studies in Race, Ethnicity, Indigeneity and Criminal Justice,
https://doi.org/10.1057/978-1-349-95807-8_5

toward legal authorities, including the police. To gain a more complete understanding of the issues of race/ethnicity, immigration, and policing in this country, one therefore cannot neglect the voices and experiences of the nation's Asian Americans.

Within the extremely heterogeneous category of Asian Americans, the largest group is that of Chinese Americans (Terrazas & Batalova, 2010). In 2011, Chinese Americans approached 4.2 million in number, constituting nearly 23% of the total Asian American population (U.S. Bureau of the Census, 2011). In a few medium and small cities in California (e.g., Monterey Park and San Marino), Chinese Americans have become the racial majority. This chapter focuses on issues of crime, victimization, contacts with the police, and assessments of the police among Chinese Americans, including both foreign-born individuals who have Chinese-born parents, and native-born Americans who claim Chinese ancestry. Presently, the population of foreign-born Chinese, who originally come from Mainland China, Hong Kong, Macau, Taiwan, and other countries in Southeast Asia that feature large populations of the Chinese diaspora, is greater than the population of U.S.-born Chinese Americans (Terrazas & Batalova, 2010).

In the following sections, we first introduce the history of Chinese immigration in the U.S., and the principal contours of contemporary Chinese American communities. We then describe the overall experience of crime and contact with the police among Chinese Americans. After that, we discuss the existing evidence regarding Chinese Americans' evaluations of the police, including both patterns and major correlates of such perceptions. Whenever relevant, literature on Asian Americans' experiences and perceptions is also reviewed.

Immigration History, Contemporary Communities, and Racial Relations

Chinese Americans have been residents in the U.S. for over two centuries. Early Chinese immigrants were mainly contract laborers working as miners and railroad builders on the West Coast. In the nineteenth century, Chinese immigrants were stereotyped as offensive, exotic, potentially dangerous and *perpetual foreigners* who could never assimilate into civilized Western culture, regardless of citizenship or duration of residence in the U.S. By the late nineteenth century, Chinese, along with other Asian groups, were broadly perceived as constituting the "yellow peril," characterized as undesirable foreigners who have a distinctive alien character generally seen as inferior, reflecting cultural traditions and practices featuring lower moral and ethical standards from those of White Americans (Yen, 2000). Even for Asian Americans who are second-plus generation (i.e., born and raised in the U.S.), they are still regarded by many non-Asian Americans as outsiders who can never fully assimilate into the American society (Kim, 1999; Lee, 1999; Lowe, 1996; Tuan, 2003).

Anti-Chinese sentiments started to grow to substantial levels when Chinese laborers began moving off White-owned plantations and mining and railroad building sites and opened their own businesses and commercial enterprises in urban areas during the late nineteenth century. This was especially the case when their low cost labor was no longer needed in the mining and railroad industries. In many cases, Chinese laborers were forced out of gold fields in the West and, while searching for life opportunities elsewhere, were increasingly seen as competitors for jobs and wages in urban areas such as San Francisco and Los Angeles. Starting as early as 1852, a number of anti-Chinese legislation and court decisions were passed in California (Chan, 1991; Hsu, 2000; Sayler, 1995; Takaki, 1998). Anti-Chinese sentiment continued to mount during the transitional history on the West Coast and numerous business associations and labor organizations in San Francisco filed a joint petition to the U.S. Congress to prohibit Chinese immigration (Chan, 1986; Lee, 2003). The California State Senate published a formal report in which it was claimed that Chinese immigrants had failed to adopt American values, habits and religious beliefs, as well as had polluted California with alien drug use and gambling activities which threatened to contaminate White Americans (Pfaelzer, 2007; Tichenor, 2002). Nefarious forms of *ethnic cleansing* and *violence* in California and in the Pacific Northwest began to take place (Chan, 1986, 1991; Pfaelzer, 2007; Saxton, 1971; Takaki, 1998). Between the 1860s and 1880s, many Chinese houses were burned to the ground and thousands of Chinese people were rounded up and purged from more than 300 communities by vigilante citizen groups working in concert with dishonest politicians while law enforcement ignored their duty to protect these citizens from such hate crimes (Pfaelzer, 2007; Saxton, 1971). Many Chinese Americans were violently herded onto railroad cars, tramp steamers, or logging rafts, marched out of town, or even killed on the spot. Most of the people participating in the killings were acquitted of any crimes through jury nullification, and most of those who were found guilty of murder only received lenient sentences (Pfaelzer, 2007).

The hostility toward Chinese immigrants reached its peak when the U.S. Congress passed the *Chinese Exclusion Act of 1882*. The *Act*, which is seen as one of the darkest moments for Chinese Americans, completely suspended the immigration of Chinese laborers and banned existing Chinese immigrants who left the U.S. (e.g., to visit family) from returning. It is the only federal legislation ever enacted into law that banned immigrants explicitly based on a specific nationality (Chan, 1991). Chinese immigrants were placed under government scrutiny and were made permanent aliens in the act by being excluded from U.S. citizenship (Gyory, 1998). Under the tremendous anti-Chinese pressure of the times, *Chinatowns* were established in major cities where Chinese immigrants could retreat into their own cultural and social colonies and regain a sense of safety in a hostile society. Less known than this history of Chinese exclusion and social marginalization, however, is the extraordinary legacy of active resistance that Chinese people showed during this period. This resistance was manifested through boycotts, petitions, and lawsuits directed toward this form of social injustice (Sayler, 1995). Altogether, Chinese immigrants filed more than 7000 lawsuits in the decade after the *1882 Act*, and eventually won the vast majority of them (Pfaelzer, 2007).

The *Chinese Exclusion Act* was repealed in 1943 and Chinese immigrants were allowed to enter the U.S. with a miniscule quota of 105 persons per year, and Chinese Americans who were resident aliens were permitted to apply for naturalization. The country's door did not fully open for Chinese until the mid-1960s when the *Immigration Act of 1965* was enacted which abolished the national origin and quota system and established the new system of allocating immigrant visas on a *first come, first served* basis (Jackson, 2006). The *1965 Act* represented a shift of American national identify from a Eurocentric to a multicultural one, bringing much more tolerance and acceptance toward non-Eurocentric immigrants—including the Chinese (Wong, 2005).

New waves of Chinese immigration began under these new circumstances. Between the 1960s and the 1980s, large numbers of Chinese from Taiwan and Hong Kong migrated to the U.S., especially to attend American public and private universities. Many former students remained, joining established professions and opening businesses and raising families in communities across the entire country. By the late 1990s, immigration from Taiwan started to decrease. Meanwhile, beginning in the 1980s and continuing up to the present, Chinese immigration has been predominantly from mainland China. Unlike their predecessors prior to 1965, many Chinese came to America no longer to fill hard labor positions, but rather as desired graduate students, professionals, and skilled technicians needed for the new knowledge-based economy. In particular, policymakers sought to attract Asians, including Chinese, for scientific and technical positions that American students had not filled (Yen, 2000). Consequently, the character of Chinese American communities has gradually transformed from urban ethnic enclaves predominately comprised of poor, uneducated laundry and restaurant owners to suburban, better-off, well-educated communities with highly valued working professionals. In addition, second-plus generation Chinese Americans interact more regularly with other racial/ethnic groups, increasing their visibility as noteworthy participants in American society. It is likely that the more open and tolerant social environment coming into existence after the civil rights movement in the 1960s has also contributed to greater acceptance and appreciation of Asian Americans in the U.S. (Yen, 2000).

Despite this growth in social standing and improved socio-economic conditions, Chinese Americans, first-generation especially, tend to live in two distinctive worlds (Logan, Zhang, & Alba, 2002; Toro-Morn & Alicea, 2004). *Uptown Chinese* professionals and entrepreneurs, who have high educational attainment, tend to work in prestigious institutions and corporations, live in safer suburban communities characterized by higher degrees of acculturation, and have lower risks of victimization. In contrast, *Downtown Chinese* workers, who generally have low educational achievement, tend to perform labor-intensive, low-skilled work in the lowest wage manufacturing and service sectors, then to live in urban ethnic enclaves with lower levels of acculturation and higher levels of crime and disorder, and are subject to greater risks of victimization. Although every racial/ethnic group has some degree of within-group differentiation, the Chinese immigrant community is broadly recognized as being more socioeconomically polarized than any of the other Asian immigrant communities in the U.S. (Min, 2006).

As with all minority populations in the U.S., race and ethnicity can be part of the "lived experience" of Chinese Americans (Feagin & Sikes, 1994). Being a Chinese can shape every aspect of a person's life and become the master status of that person (Cose, 1993). Chinese Americans are associated with stereotypes that are commonly shared among Asian groups. Some of these ascribed characteristics include physical attributes (e.g., slanted eyes), personality traits (e.g., industrious, workaholic, dull), societal roles (e.g., occupation), or specific behaviors (Lee, Vue, Seklecki, & Ma, 2007). The two primary stereotypes of Asian Americans—"forever foreigners" and "model minorities"—may have profound implications for Chinese Americans' relationships with and attitudes toward the police.

The image of *forever foreigners* for Chinese Americans can position them as "outsiders who do not have a stake in American society and therefore constitute the sources of moral panics and social anxieties" (Aguirre & Lio, 2008, p. 1). Such an image also implies that Chinese Americans are less loyal to this country (Lee et al., 2007). Further, due to their out-group status (Blumer, 1958), they may be regarded as alien competitors for scarce resources, threats to the existing racial and economic order, and undeserving of the rights and privileges of dominant groups. Unfortunately, although many Asian Americans have experienced adverse stereotyping, prejudicial attitudes, discrimination in social and economic affairs, underemployment in the workforce, and a lack of upward organizational mobility vis-à-vis administrative roles, these commonplace negative experiences are neither widely recognized nor well understood by members of the dominant society. Dismissive and degrading comments such as "At least you are not black," or "You should be grateful that you are not black" can often be heard directed toward Asian Americans (Kim, 1998, p. 4). These comments reflect the particular, perhaps unique, kind of racism that Asian Americans can acknowledge and should challenge.

Meanwhile, the *model minority* image depicts Chinese Americans as a non-White group that has achieved upward social mobility and societal acceptance through its hard work and its adherence to traditional family-oriented values. This stereotype surfaced during the 1960s when the social problem of racial inequality was highlighted and minorities began to vigorously challenge the fundamental fairness and dispensation of justice of the American society. Asian Americans were used as an example to question the claims raised of institutional racism, and to reinforce the legitimacy of the White power structure and the values it putatively represented. **Quiet, docile, hardworking, and excelling both at school and work** were the stereotype images of Asian Americans which were prominent during these troubled times, traits that suggest that Asians are able to overcome their minority status and realize the American dream and hence substantiate the claim that American society is fair and just—offering "with justice and liberty for all" of its citizens.

This seemingly positive stereotype has some negative consequences, however. For example, although many Chinese Americans do not conform to the model minority stereotype, they are not eligible to be included in educational and employment programs designed to help disadvantaged minorities. In addition, "while being encouraged to feel superior to African Americans, Asian Americans are being positioned in a racial hierarchy meant to perpetuate white privilege at the expense of both Asian and African Americans" (Kim, 1998, p. 4). Moreover, the model minority stereotype can often elevate racial tensions among minority groups (Yen, 2000). Other minority groups, being blamed for not having achieved the same levels of economic and social success, develop a sense of competition with and animosity towards Asian Americans. The 1992 attacks made upon Asian-owned stores by African Americans during the Los Angeles riots to the wake of the beating of Rodney King illustrate the perceived White-Asian solidarity by many Blacks (Yen, 2000). It is widely believed that discrimination is truly grounded on Black–White race relations, and that Asian Americans cannot be regarded as an "oppressed minority" in American society (Morishima, 1981).

The Los Angeles riots of 1992 represent the nation's first instance of multiracial riots, and serve as a manifestation of inter-minority conflicts that have emerged in many American cities (Kim & Lee, 2001). While a White-Black dichotomous framework for the analysis of minority issues is criticized frequently in the research literature and public press alike (Alcoff, 2003; Perea, 1997; Schmitt, 2001), Asian Americans continue to be viewed by many scholars and commentators as similar to Whites vis-à-vis their status in the American power structure. Claims that Asian Americans are adversely affected by racial prejudices in the criminal justice system are often poorly received, by both Asians and non-Asians (Yen, 2000). Indeed, while roughly 40% of Asian Americans reported having personally experienced discrimination (Bobo, Zubrinsky, Johnson, & Oliver, 1994; Lee, 2000; Lien, Conway, Lee, & Wong, 2001; Uhlaner, 1991), very few Americans, Asian Americans included, feel that Asian Americans as a group face special obstacles (Bobo & Johnson, 2000; Lee, 2000; Uhlaner, 1991). These complicated interracial relationships in the U.S. can shape the life experiences of Chinese immigrants, their self-images, and others' perceptions of them, and influence their relationships with formal social institutions—including the police.

Experience with Crime and Criminal Justice

An Asian presence is often missing from the crime and criminal justice literature. Asian Americans, like other citizens, can and do get involved in the criminal justice system as law enforcers, victims/offenders, or service requesters, yet none of these roles and their associated experiences have been studied in any depth. Asian Americans are severely underrepresented in the profession of policing. Data from the law enforcement agencies of Los Angeles County and Orange County, California, showed the great extent of underrepresentation of Asian Americans in police forces; their underrepresentation far exceeds that of the Blacks and Latinos in the high-minority southern California area (Schroedel, J., Frisch, S., August, R., Kalogris, C., & Perkins, A., 1994).

With respect to victimization, secondary data do not always have a separate response category of Asian Americans when inquiring into race-based patterns of incidence. Asian Americans were often included in the "other races" category in many official research reports. Nationwide, the Federal Bureau of Investigation's *Uniform Crime Reports* (UCR) indicated that Asians are underrepresented in victimization. The *National Crime Victimization Survey* (NCVS) data revealed that Asian women have the lowest risk of victimization of any group, but the risks increased substantially when Asian women were employed and lived in female-headed households (Dugan & Apel, 2003). Some state-level data suggest that certain types of criminal victimizations among Asian Americans have been on the rise in more recent decades. Between 1970 and 1993, for instance, Asians in California experienced a similar homicide rate as that of non-Hispanic Whites, but since the 1990s Asians' risks of homicide victimization have become significantly greater than those of Whites (Chu & Sorenson, 1996).

Official data are likely to underestimate the extent of victimization of Asian Americans, especially foreign-borns, as underreporting of crime is particularly widespread among this population (Coleman & Moynihan, 1996). Various factors may contribute to the well documented underreporting phenomenon. For example, coming from an authoritarian state with weak legal traditions, immigrants from mainland China may have poor legal consciousness and hold low trust in formal institutions (Peerenboom, 2002; Turner, Feinerman, & Guy, 2000), making them less likely to resist victimization assertively and pursue grievances through appeals to the police. Also, since the police in China are often corrupt and abuse their power (Sun & Wu, 2010), Chinese immigrants may not think the U.S. police can be fair or helpful in addressing their needs. Further, as Chinese culture strongly emphasizes social harmony and collectivism, some Chinese Americans may avoid bringing their problems to the attention of authorities, as they would view official intervention as seriously undermining the honor of their family and the broader community. Additionally, Chinese immigrants who are new to American society may have substantial language barriers and lack working knowledge about American laws and the legal system, hindering both their willingness and **ability** to report a crime. Finally, undocumented immigrants and their family members or close friends may be especially reluctant to have official contact with the police because of their heightened fear of detention and possible deportation (Davis & Erez, 1996; Herbst & Walker, 2001).

With the issue of underreporting in mind, self-report data have shown that Asian American communities have commonly experienced crimes involving family members, such as domestic violence (Chin, 1990, 1996; Postner, 1988; Song & Hurysz, 1995), child abuse (Chang, Rhee, & Weaver, 2006; Gilligan & Akhtar, 2006; Maker, Shah, & Agha, 2005), and elderly mistreatment (Moon, Tomita, & Jung, 2001). These crimes probably have less impact on people's attitudes toward the police than street crimes, such as gang-related extortion and robberies. Research evidence indicates that gang extortion is actually one of the most prevalent crimes in urban Chinese enclaves, with over 90% of the businesses in Manhattan's Chinatown reporting having experienced extortion by Chinese gangs (Chin, 1990, 1996). Chinese immigrants who have to work late as factory workers and take-out restaurant deliverers, and who do not have a bank account and keep cash at home, are disproportionately likely to be targets of robbery, home invasion robbery, kidnapping, and theft. It is estimated that about half of undocumented Chinese immigrants in New York City Chinatown had been victimized at least once since their arrival in the U.S., mostly by common thieves (Chin, 1999). Specifically, 32% had been robbed in the subway, and 10% had been robbed at home, but only 18% of the crime victims experiencing these crimes against them reported the crimes in question to the police (Chin, 1999).

The model minority stereotype, as aforementioned, can impede people's recognition of Asian Americans as crime victims in general. It can also undermine public awareness of ongoing anti-Asian sentiment and racially motivated crimes against Asian Americans in specific. Tragedies such as Vincent Chin's murder in Detroit in 1982 show how easy it is to deny Asian victims a true victim status, and how difficult it is to secure a conviction under hate crime statutes for violence committed against Asian Americans (Yen, 2000). Vincent Chin, a 27-year-old Chinese American in Detroit, was beaten to death by two white autoworkers. The crime was racially motivated due to anti-Japanese sentiments arising from layoffs in the auto industry with the rise of the Japanese auto industry. Wayne County Circuit Court Judge Charles Kaufman sentenced the two offenders after their conviction for manslaughter very leniently; the offenders were given $3000 fines and 3-year probation sentences, with **no prison time**. This decision angered Asian Americans, both in Detroit and around the entire country. Asian Americans were united for the first time across ethnic and socioeconomic lines to form a pan-Asian identity and to initiate a civil rights movement for the promotion of justice and fair treatment for Asian people in the U.S.

Since the mid-1990s, there has been a noticeable increase in hate crimes and racial attacks against Asian Americans (Fletcher, 1999, August 29; Noble, 1995, December 13; Sun, 1997, September 9). Many of these hate crimes are perpetrated against Asian American children, often by other children (*USA Today*, 2005, November 13). The anti-Asian American incidents include the use of racial slurs, physical attacks, vandalism of cars and graffiti, intimidation, robberies, and even murders (Kitano & Daniels, 2001; Stewart, 2001, January 25). The *forever foreigner* stereotype, unfortunately, may increase the likelihood of acquittal in cases involving Asian American victims. The Steffen Wong case, for example, where Wong was shot by his neighbor when he was entering his own home, resulted in an acquittal of the neighbor as the jurors reasoned that the defendant acted in self-defense because he believed that the "oriental" must know martial arts (*State v. Simon*, 1982). The Wong case illustrates how the image of Asian men as dangerous foreigners can help "justify" an unjust killing under the pretext of self-defense (Yen, 2000).

In terms of police contact, Asian Americans are found to have fewer encounters with the police than other racial groups, regardless of offending status (Sharp & Budd, 2005). Mixed results have been reported about the volume of traffic stops involving Asian Americans, which represent the most common reason for public–police contacts. Two studies based on official data collected from Sacramento, California and Minneapolis, Minnesota found that Asian Americans were underrepresented in police vehicle stops and were less likely to be detained, arrested, and booked by the police following these stops compared to White, Black, and non-White Hispanic Americans (Council on Crime and Justice, 2001; Greenwald, 2001). Another statewide study conducted in Kentucky, however, found that Asian American drivers were stopped in lower proportion for compliance violations, yet were more frequently stopped for traffic violations than other racial/ethnic groups (Wilson, 2001). Analyzing more than 10,000 traffic stops on a college campus, a fourth study revealed that Asian drivers were more likely than other racial groups, including African Americans, to receive legal sanctions during traffic stops (Moon & Corley, 2007). This finding was unexpected given that Asians were generally less likely to exhibit hostility and aggression toward the police than other citizens. It is possible that poor language hindered effective communication between officers and Asian drivers, resulting in more frequent issuing of sanctions against Asian Americans. It is also possible that Moon and Corley's study was conducted on a college campus, with stops involving mostly young adults and a high proportion of foreign-born Asian students. Compared to the general American public, these young Asian drivers are likely to be less experienced in driving.

Empirical evidence specifically on Chinese Americans is even rarer in the research literature. Survey data collected from 300 or so Chinese immigrants in New York City, Philadelphia, and Delaware revealed that 41% of the survey respondents reported having at least one encounter with the police during the period 2007–2008 (Wu, Triplett, & Sun, 2012), which was significantly higher than the average national rate of 17% among the general public reported by the *2008 Police–Public Contact Survey* (Eith & Durose, 2011). The majority of Chinese immigrants' contacts with the police (57%) were initiated by the police. Among those who had recent contacts with the police, over half had contacts due to traffic law violations and/or accidents (Wu et al., 2012). This proportion is in line with statistics from the *2008 Police–Public Contact Survey*, which indicated that 59% of the surveyed American residents age 16 or older had their most recent contacts with the police in connection with traffic-related circumstances (Eith & Durose, 2011).

Chinese Americans' Attitudes Toward the Police

A small number of studies have examined Asian Americans' perceptions of the police. A comparison of Vietnamese and Latino evaluations of the police in Garden Grove, CA revealed that Vietnamese residents expressed more favorable views of the police than did their counterpart Latino residents (Torres & Vogel, 2001). Also using data from Southern California, another study found that Chinese immigrants were demonstrably more fearful of crime and had significantly greater concerns of police prejudice against minority residents than Vietnamese refugees in the Los Angeles area (Song, 1992). Comparing public attitudes toward the police across four racial/ethnic groups, Whites, Blacks, Latinos, and Asians, a recent study found that in two evaluative areas, those of police harassment and racial profiling, Hispanic and Asian Americans occupied an "in-between position" on the vertical attitudinal scale, expressing more positive views than Blacks and more negative views than Whites (Wu, 2014). In two other evaluative areas, those of constructive problem-solving and police officer bias, however, Asian, Hispanic, and White Americans shared similar ratings, all being significantly more favorable than those of Blacks. Based on these results, the author suggested that a racial/ethnic hierarchy of White–Asian–Black, White–Hispanic–Black, or White–Asian–Hispanic–Black, along with the color line, in explaining public satisfaction with the police, is too simplistic. The complexity of policing and the multi-dimensional nature of public assessments of the police make the racial/ethnic group positions in determining such evaluations highly dynamic.

A growing number of studies have investigated Chinese Americans' opinions on the police. Survey data collected from over 300 Chinese Americans on the East Coast revealed that the majority of the respondents had positive views on the police (Wu, Sun, & Smith, 2011). Eighty-four percent of the respondents reported being generally satisfied with the police who served their local communities. This finding was largely consistent with the results from nation-wide opinion polls. For example, the *Criminal Victimization and Perceptions of Community Safety in 12 U.S. Cities Survey* asked over 11,000 Americans exactly the same question on global satisfaction with the police and found that 21.6% of the respondents reported "very satisfied" and 65.7% reported "satisfied" with local police (Wu et al., 2011).

Regarding specific attitudes toward the police, available evidence indicated that Chinese Americans have favorable evaluations of **some** aspects of police performance, but not others. For example, Chinese immigrants gave high ratings to officer demeanor, integrity and effectiveness of local police (Wu et al., 2011), but there was widespread belief that racialized policing existed (Wu, Smith, & Sun, 2013). Between 60 and 70% of the respondents either strongly agreed or agreed that racial/ethnic minorities, poor, or non-English-speaking people were treated worse than Whites, wealthy, or English-speaking people by the police (Wu et al., 2013). A perception that the police treat Chinese unfairly in comparison to Whites was especially prevalent among the respondents. Thus, while the majority of Chinese immigrants think highly of the U.S. police in general, and have faith in police honesty and effectiveness, they are less positive about police providing equal treatment to all of America's diverse social groups. Similar results were reported in a comparative study of Chinese immigrants in New York City and Toronto (Chu & Song, 2015). The researchers found that the two groups displayed no difference in their assessments of police efficacy and adequacy of protection, yet the New York City respondents were more likely to perceive police prejudice than their Toronto counterparts. This attitudinal difference may be attributed to different policing styles—while "the Toronto police have advocated community policing and embraced the philosophy of multiculturalism...in response to a high crime rate and the post-9/11 effect, the aggressive policing approach adopted in NYC may somehow affect the police-Chinese community relationship" (Chu & Song, 2015, p. 420).

Worth mentioning, this pervasive impression of police bias among Chinese immigrants resembles attitudinal patterns exhibited among other minority groups in the U.S. Several studies have found that while the majority of Whites generally believe that the police are racially neutral and treat different racial/ethnic groups equally before the law, most African Americans, and to a lesser extent, Hispanics, hold the belief that racial/ethnic minorities are subject to police racial bias and injustice (Hagan & Albonetti, 1982; Henderson, Cullen, Cao, Browning, & Kopache, 1997; Rice & Piquero, 2005; Weitzer & Tuch, 2005). Chinese immigrants in Canada also expressed similar concerns about police bias. One study found that 56% of the Chinese respondents in Toronto agreed that "Blacks are treated differently than Whites" and 46% agreed that "Chinese are treated differently than Whites"

(Wortley, 1996), and another documented that about 50% of the surveyed Chinese immigrants in Toronto believed that police treated Blacks worse than Whites, and that police treated Chinese worse than Whites (Wortley & Owusu-Bempah, 2009). All of these percentages nevertheless were lower than what were found (60–70%) in Wu and colleagues' (2013) study, indicating greater resentment toward police bias among Chinese immigrants in the U.S than their counterparts in Canada.

Researchers have explored several groups of factors that may influence Chinese immigrants' perceptions of the police. These factors tap into background characteristics, experiences with crime and the police, exposure to media reports, neighborhood contexts, and immigrant-specific variables such as language proficiency, length of stay and perceptions of home country police. Among them, demographic characteristics, such as age and social class, are often found non-significant in determining Chinese immigrants' views on the police (Chu, Song, & Dombrink, 2005; Wu, 2009). Gender sometimes plays a role though, with females displaying lower levels of both global satisfaction with the police and specific satisfaction with officer demeanor than males (Wu et al., 2011).

Experience with crime and contact with the police are frequently predictive of Chinese immigrants' attitudes toward the police. Chinese New Yorkers who had prior contact with the police, who rated the police as useful when called for assistance, who expressed less fear of crime, and who were not victims of crime were more likely to view the police as effective (Chu et al., 2005). Those Chinese New Yorkers who did not have prior contact with the police and who rated the police as helpful in those encounters when called for assistance also expressed greater respect for the police.

Police performance during a specific contact has played a salient role in shaping Chinese immigrants' global satisfaction with the police. It is found that whether or not U.S. Chinese immigrants had recent police contact, either personal or vicarious, did not influence their overall satisfaction with the police (Wu et al., 2011). However, among Chinese immigrants who had recent police contacts, those who were more satisfied with their most recent police contacts also evaluated local police in general more positively (Wu et al., 2011). Similarly, among a sample of Chinese immigrants in San Francisco perceptions of recent police contact were found to have a significant relationship to general perceptions of the police (Chu & Hung, 2010). Those who were satisfied with their recent contact, even if the contact entailed receiving a traffic ticket from the police, displayed more positive views toward the police (Chu & Hung, 2010).

The way police handled the case during the encounter, therefore, matters more than the occurrence of the encounter in determining satisfaction. A strong connection between evaluations of officer demeanor and perceived police bias was also observed. When Chinese immigrants considered police officers to be friendly, respectful, and communicative, they held a stronger belief that the police will uphold the ideals of equal justice (Wu et al., 2013). These patterns echo the argument of procedural justice theory that how police officers interact with citizens, including their manner, attitudes, and behaviors, have important implications for public sentiments toward and evaluations of the police (Reitzel, Rice, & Piquero, 2004; Thurman & Reisig, 1996; Tyler, 1990).

Compared to police contact, experience with crime and fear of crime play a lesser role in shaping Chinese immigrants' perceptions of the police. Neither personal victimization nor fear of crime influenced Chinese immigrants' global satisfaction with the police or specific evaluations of officer demeanor, police integrity, effectiveness, and bias (Wu et al., 2011, 2013). Studies conducted in Toronto showed that while violent victimization does not affect Chinese Canadians' perceptions of police bias (Wortley & Owusu-Bempah, 2009), fear of crime at night is significantly linked to their perceptions of police prejudice against Asians (Chu & Song, 2008).

Another experiential factor, indirect in nature, has been examined in some studies. Media exposure to police misconduct is found to exert a significant negative effect on Chinese immigrants' global satisfaction and specific evaluations of police bias, effectiveness, integrity and demeanor (Wu et al., 2011, 2013). This negative effect of media coverage of police misconduct is not unique to Chinese immigrants; researchers have found it to be present among other groups, such as African Americans and Hispanics (Weitzer & Tuch, 2005). People seem to be much more likely to remember, and be influenced by, negative experiences than positive ones, a phenomenon which is referred to as the "negative bias effect" (Weitzer & Tuch, 2006).

In face of the significant media influence, a few publicized incidents of police allegedly committing brutality and racial profiling against Asian Americans may have a lingering negative effect on Chinese Americans' opinions on the police (Wu et al., 2011). For example, in the Yong Xin Huang case, the 16-year-old honor student Huang was shot in the head by the police when he was playing with a pellet gun and showing no sign of resistance (Hevesi, 1995). In the Michael Cho case, the 25-year-old artist Cho was shot multiple times by the police when he posed no imminent threat to police officers or others (*Los Angeles Times*, 2008, February 11). Cases such as these may become an especially important source of indirect experience with the police for Chinese Americans.

Some contextual/structural variables have emerged as significant predictors of Chinese immigrants' attitudes toward the police. Chinese immigrants who lived in neighborhoods with higher degrees of collective efficacy and lower levels of crime and disorder tended to view local police more positively (Wu et al., 2011). These results add to a growing number of studies that found the supremacy of neighborhood contextual characteristics in predicting American residents' satisfaction with the police (Dai & Johnson, 2009; Reisig & Parks, 2000; Sampson & Jeglum-Bartusch, 1998; Wu, Sun, & Triplett, 2009). In addition, Chinese Americans in rural or suburban areas viewed their local police more favorably than their counterparts in urban areas (Wu et al., 2011), which is consistent with the results from the general American public (e.g., Kusow, Wilson, & Martin, 1997; Weitzer & Tuch, 2005).

Finally, a few researchers have taken immigrant-specific factors into account when examining Chinese immigrants' perceptions of the police, given that a large proportion of Chinese Americans are foreign-born. So far, very little research has actually asked the basic question of whether native- and foreign-born Chinese residents in the U.S. share similar or divergent views on the police. One study found that foreign-born Chinese displayed a significantly lower level of satisfaction with police effectiveness and demeanor than U.S.-born Chinese Americans (Wu et al., 2011), but more research is needed to investigate this issue.

Popular belief tends to hold that assimilation affects immigrants' perceptions of the police. Surprisingly, the existing evidence shows that language proficiency, a key indicator of assimilation, is not predictive of Chinese immigrants' perceptions of the police. Language proficiency was not significantly related either to Chinese immigrants' perceptions of police anti-Chinese bias or the exercise of prejudice in their work (Wu et al., 2013; Chu & Song, 2008), respect for the police, or assessments of police effectiveness and rapid response (Chu & Song, 2015). However, communication barriers between the police and immigrants, which go beyond language problems, can undermine public satisfaction with the police. A Chinese Canadian sample revealed that although English-speaking ability did not affect Chinese immigrants' perceptions of police prejudice against Asians, those who considered poor communication a serious issue in police-Chinese interactions in Toronto were more inclined to believe that police discriminated against Asians (Chu & Song, 2008).

Inconsistent results have been found regarding the effects of another key indicator of assimilation—namely, length of stay in the host country. While some researchers found no significant effects of length of residence on Chinese immigrants' perceptions of police prejudice, effectiveness in crime control, or provision of adequate protection (Chu & Song, 2015), others discovered some curvilinear effects of length of residence on Chinese immigrants' perceptions of police bias (Wu et al., 2013). Interestingly, newcomers who have been in this country for less than three years had the most positive views on police equal treatment. In contrast, Chinese immigrants who have resided in the U.S. for a median period of time (4–14 years) had the least positive views concerning police provision of equal treatment to citizens. Yet, for the long-term Chinese immigrants (longer than 14 years), their perceptions of police bias were no longer more negative than those of the new-arrivals.

It is speculated that these attitudinal variations reflect the ongoing assimilation process of Chinese immigrants in this country (Wu et al., 2013). The positive views of newcomers may be associated with the voluntary nature of post-1965 Chinese immigration. Many more recent Chinese immigrants tend to have positive expectations upon their arrival, seeing this country as a symbol of equality and opportunity. Staying longer, however, they apparently experience more cultural shock and social conflict, recognizing the strained racial relations present, including police-minority relations, and gradually develop a stronger sense of racial distinctiveness and rights consciousness. Then, when immigrants have stayed in the country for an extensive period of time, although remaining critical about the police, they no longer tend to perceive the police significantly more negatively than newcomers. Instead, with improved socioeconomic status and greater degrees of assimilation, longer-term residents can feel more confident in encounters with legal authorities, and more trustful of such formal social institutions as the police. In addition, there is the possibility that long-term immigrants stay longer at least in part because they are satisfied with the way the U.S. government functions, including the performance of the criminal justice system.

Immigrants' perception of their home country police is another key variable that deserves more attention. Chinese immigrants who perceived home police as effective held more positive assessments of police effectiveness in dealing with crime in the U.S. and Canada (Chu & Song, 2015). Chinese immigrants who expressed more positive evaluations of home country police in terms of demeanor, honesty, and effectiveness were also more satisfied with the effectiveness and integrity of the U.S. police (Wu et al., 2011). These findings were consistent with the results of a study on Korean Americans showing a positive link between perceptions of home country and host country police (Pogrebin & Poole, 1990).

Finally, there is some noteworthy evidence pointing to an important connection between Chinese immigrants' evaluations of U.S. immigration authorities' job performance and their assessments of the performance of their local police. Among Chinese immigrants who had recent contacts with immigration officials, those who thought poorly of immigration officials and their services also displayed significantly less favorable attitudes toward their local police (Wu et al., 2011). It is possible that immigrants are confused about the differences between federal immigration authorities and local police officer (oftentimes plain-clothed) (Skogan, 2009). It can be especially difficult for the children of immigrants to distinguish between local police and immigration authorities (Chaudry et al., 2010). Immigrant children (most of whom are American citizens) who witnessed parental arrest and who suffered parental separation may also develop great fear of the police and no longer trust the police (Chaudry et al., 2010). These concerns elucidate the importance of having sound immigration policies in this country (Wu et al., 2011).

Summary

As the largest Asian group in the U.S., Chinese Americans have a long and, at times, very thorny and strenuous path of immigration and acculturation in this country. The contemporary Chinese American communities resulting from the post-1965 wave of immigration tend to develop and expand rapidly, with a simultaneous trend of diversification and even polarization in socioeconomic status and local residence area. Chinese Americans are commonly subject to the stereotypes of *forever foreigners* and *model minorities*, both of which may complicate their positions in the racial relations in American society, and their relations with the American police.

With respect to perceptions of the police, existing evidence suggests that Chinese Americans in general have high levels of global satisfaction with the police. They are, however, more positive about some specific aspects of police performance, such as police officer effectiveness, integrity, and demeanor, than others, such as equal treatment of all persons. Predictors of Chinese immigrants' perceptions of the police include both universal traits and immigrant-specific variables. Experiential and contextual variables, such as police contact, media effects, and neighborhood conditions, are found closely related to Chinese immigrants' assessments of the police. Some immigrant-specific variables, such as length of residence, perceptions of home country police, and evaluations of immigration officials, have also been demonstrated to influence Chinese immigrants' perceptions of the U.S. police in certain ways.

References

Aguirre, A., Jr., & Lio, S. (2008). Spaces of mobilization: The Asian American/Pacific Islander struggle for social justice. *Social Justice, 35,* 1–17.

Alcoff, L. (2003). Latino/as, Asian Americans, and the Black–White binary. *The Journal of Ethics, 7,* 5–27.

Blumer, H. (1958). Race prejudice as a sense of group position. *Pacific Sociological Review, 1,* 3–7.

Bobo, L., & Johnson, D. (2000). Racial attitudes in a prismatic metropolis: Mapping identity, stereotypes, competition, and views on affirmative action. In L. Bobo, M. Oliver, J. Johnson, & A. Valenzuela (Eds.), *Prismatic metropolis: Inequality in Los Angeles* (pp. 81–162). New York, NY: Russell Sage Foundation.

Bobo, L., Zubrinsky, C. L., Johnson, J. H., Jr., & Oliver, M. L. (1994). Public opinion before and after a spring of discontent. In M. Baldassare (Ed.), *The Los Angeles riots: Lessons for the urban future* (pp. 103–133). Boulder, CO: Westview.

Chan, S. (1986). *This bittersweet soil: Chinese in California agriculture, 1860–1910.* Berkeley, CA: University of California Press.

Chan, S. (1991). *Asian Americans: An interpretive history.* Boston, MA: Twayne Publishers.

Chang, J., Rhee, S., & Weaver, D. (2006). Characteristics of child abuse in immigrant Korean families and correlates of placement decisions. *Child Abuse and Neglect, 30,* 881–891.

Chaudry, A., Capps, R., Pedroza, J., Castaneda, R., Santos, R., & Scott, M. (2010). *Facing our future, children in the aftermath of immigration enforcement.* Washington, DC: The Urban Institute.

Chin, K. (1990). *Chinese subculture and criminality.* Westport, CT: Greenwood.

Chin, K. (1996). *Chinatown gangs: Extortion, enterprise, and ethnicity.* New York, NY: Oxford University Press.

Chin, K. (1999). *Smuggled Chinese: Clandestine immigration to the United States.* Philadelphia, PA: Temple University Press.

Chu, D., & Hung, L. (2010). Chinese immigrants' attitudes toward the police in San Francisco. *Policing: An International Journal of Police Strategies and Management, 33,* 621–643.

Chu, D., & Song, J. (2008). Chinese immigrants' perceptions of the police in Toronto, Canada. *Policing: An International Journal of Police Strategies and Management, 31,* 610–630.

Chu, D., & Song, J. (2015). A comparison of Chinese immigrants' perceptions of the police in New York City and Toronto. *Crime & Delinquency, 61,* 402–427.

Chu, D., Song, J., & Dombrink, J. (2005). Chinese immigrants' perceptions of the police in New York City. *International Criminal Justice Review, 15,* 101–114.

Chu, L., & Sorenson, S. (1996). Trends in California homicide: 1970–1993. *Western Journal of Medicine, 165,* 119–125.

Coleman, C., & Moynihan, J. (1996). *Understanding crime data: Haunted by the dark figure.* Maidenhead, Berkshire: Open University Press.

Cose, E. (1993). *The rage of a privileged class.* New York, NY: Harper Perennial.

Council on Crime and Justice. (2001). *Minneapolis police traffic stops and driver's race analysis and recommendations.* Minneapolis, MN: Author.

Dai, M., & Johnson, R. (2009). Is neighborhood context a confounder? Exploring the effects of citizen race and neighborhood context on satisfaction with the police. *Policing: An International Journal of Police Strategies and Management, 32,* 595–612.

Davis, R. C., & Erez, E. (1996). *Immigrant population as victims: Toward a multicultural criminal justice system.* New York, NY: Victim Service Agency.

Dugan, L., & Apel, R. (2003). An exploratory study of the violent victimization of women: Race/ethnicity and situational context. *Criminology, 41,* 959–980.

Eith, C., & Durose, M. (2011). *Contacts between police and the public, 2008.* Washington, DC: US Department of Justice, Bureau of Justice Statistics.

Feagin, J., & Sikes, M. (1994). *Living with racism: The black middle class experience.* Boston, MA: Beacon.

Federal Bureau of Investigation. (2015). *2015 Crime in the United States: Estimated number of arrests.* Uniform Crime Report. Accessed February 9, 2018 at https://ucr.fbi.gov/crime-in-the-u.s/2015/crime-in-the-u.s.-2015/tables/table-29.

Fletcher, M. (1999, August 27). Asian American vigil decries hate crimes: Violence often unnoted, activists say. *The Washington Post,* p. A18.

Gilligan, P., & Akhtar, S. (2006). Cultural barriers to the disclosure of child sexual abuse in Asian communities: Listening to what women say. *British Journal of Social Work, 36,* 1361–1377.

Greenwald, H. (2001). *Police vehicle stops in Sacramento, California.* Sacramento, CA: City of Sacramento. Accessed November 7, 2017 at http://www.hhs.csus.edu/Homepages/CJ/GutierrezR/SacPD.pdf.

Grieco, E. (2010). *Race and Hispanic origin of the foreign-born population in the United States: 2007*. Washington, DC: U.S. Bureau of the Census.

Gyory, A. (1998). *Closing the gate: Race, politics, and the Chinese Exclusion Act*. Chapel Hill, NC: University of North Carolina Press.

Hagan, J., & Albonetti, C. (1982). Race, class and the perception of criminal injustice in America. *American Journal of Sociology, 88*, 329–355.

Henderson, M., Cullen, F., Cao, L., Browning, S., & Kopache, R. (1997). The impact of race on perceptions of criminal injustice. *Journal of Criminal Justice, 25*, 447–462.

Herbst, L., & Walker, S. (2001). Language barriers in the delivery of police services: A study of police and Hispanic interactions in a Midwestern city. *Journal of Criminal Justice, 29*, 329–340.

Hevesi, D. (1995, May 17). No indictment for officer who shot Brooklyn youth. *New York Times*. Accessed November 11, 2017 at http://query.nytimes.com/gst/fullpage.html?res=990CE2DA163DF934A25756C0A962958260.

Hsu, M. (2000). *Dreaming of gold, dreaming of home: Transnationalism and migration between the United States and South China, 1882–1943*. Stanford, CA: Stanford University Press.

Jackson, M. (2006). *Policing in a diverse society: Another American dilemma*. Durham, NC: Carolina Academic Press.

Kim, C. (1999). The racial triangulation of Asian Americans. *Politics and Society, 27*, 105–138.

Kim, E. (1998). "At least you're not black": Asian Americans in U.S. race relations. *Social Justice, 25*, 3–12.

Kim, J., & Lee, T. (2001). Interracial politics: Asian Americans and other communities of color. *PS: Political Science and Politics, 34*, 631–637.

Kitano, H., & Daniels, R. (2001). *Asian Americans: Emerging minorities*. Upper Saddle River, NJ: Prentice-Hall.

Kusow, A., Wilson, L., & Martin, D. (1997). Determinants of citizen satisfaction with the police: The effects of residential location. *Policing: An International Journal of Police Strategy and Management, 20*, 655–664.

Lee, E. (2003). *At America's gates: Chinese immigration during the exclusion era, 1882–1943*. Chapel Hill, NC: University of North Carolina Press.

Lee, R. (1999). *Oriental: Asian Americans in popular culture*. Philadelphia, PA: Temple University Press.

Lee, T. (2000). Racial attitudes and the color line(s) at the close of the twentieth century. In P. Ong (Ed.), *The state of Asian Pacific America, volume IV: Transforming race relations* (pp. 103–158). Los Angeles, CA: LEAP Asian Pacific American Public Policy Institute and UCLA.

Lee, Y., Vue, S., Seklecki, R., & Ma, Y. (2007). How did Asian Americans respond to negative stereotypes and hate crimes? *Americans Behavioral Scientist, 51,* 271–293.

Lien, P., Conway, M., Lee, T., & Wong, J. (2001). The pilot Asian American political survey: Summary report. In J. Lai & D. Nakanishi (Eds.), *The national Asian Pacific American political almanac, 2001–2002* (pp. 80–95). Los Angeles, CA: UCLA Asian American Studies Center.

Logan, J., Zhang, W., & Alba, R. (2002). Immigrant enclaves and ethnic communities in New York and Los Angeles. *American Sociological Review, 67,* 299–322.

Lopez, G., Ruiz, N., & Patten, E. (2017). *Key facts about Asian Americans, a diverse and growing population.* Pew Research Center. Accessed February 9, 2018 at http://www.pewresearch.org/fact-tank/2017/09/08/key-facts-about-asian-americans/.

Los Angeles Times. (2008, February 11). *Killing angers community.* Accessed November 11, 2017 at http://articles.latimes.com/2008/feb/11/local/me-cho11.

Lowe, L. (1996). *On Asian American cultural politics.* Durham: Duke University Press.

Maker, A., Shah, P., & Agha, Z. (2005). Child physical abuse: Prevalence, characteristics, predictors, and beliefs about parent-child violence in South Asia, middle eastern, East Asian, and Latina women in the United States. *Journal of Interpersonal Violence, 20,* 1406–1428.

Min, P. (2006). *Asian Americans: Contemporary trends and issues.* Thousand Oaks, CA: Pine Forge Press.

Moon, A., Tomita, S., & Jung, K. (2001). Elder mistreatment among four Asian American groups: An exploratory study on tolerance, victim blaming and attitudes toward third-party intervention. *Journal of Gerontological Social Work, 36,* 153–169.

Moon, B., & Corley, C. (2007). Driving across campus: Assessing the impact of drivers' race, and gender on police traffic enforcement actions. *Journal of Criminal Justice, 35,* 29–37.

Morishima, J. (1981). Special employment issues for Asian Americans. *Public Personnel Management, 10,* 384–392.

Noble, K. (1995, December 13). Attacks against Asian Americans are rising. *The New York Times,* pp. A16, B13.

Peerenboom, R. (2002). *China's long march toward the rule of law.* Cambridge, UK: Cambridge University Press.

Perea, J. (1997). The Black/White binary paradigm of race: The normal science of American racial thought. *California Law Review, 85,* 127–172.

Pfaelzer, J. (2007). *Driven out: The Forgotten War against Chinese Americans.* Berkeley, CA: University of California Press.

Pogrebin, M., & Poole, E. (1990). Cultural conflict and crime in the Korean American community. *Criminal Justice Policy Review, 4,* 69–78.

Postner, G. (1988). *Warlords of crime.* New York, NY: Penguin Books.

Reisig, M., & Parks, R. (2000). Experience, quality of life, and neighborhood context: A hierarchical analysis of satisfaction with police. *Justice Quarterly, 17,* 607–630.

Reitzel, J., Rice, S., & Piquero, A. (2004). Lines and shadows: Perceptions of racial profiling and the Hispanic experience. *Journal of Criminal Justice, 32,* 607–616.

Rice, S., & Piquero, A. (2005). Perceptions of discrimination and justice in New York City. *Policing: An International Journal of Police Strategies & Management, 28,* 98–117.

Sampson, R., & Jeglum-Bartusch, D. (1998). Legal cynicism and (subcultural?) tolerance of deviance: The neighborhood context of racial differences. *Law and Society Review, 32,* 777–804.

Saxton, A. (1971). *The indispensable enemy: Labor and the anti-Chinese movement in California.* Berkeley, CA: University of California Press.

Sayler, L. (1995). *Laws harsh as tigers.* Chapel Hill, NC: University of North Carolina Press.

Schmitt, E. (2001, March 13). For 7 million people in census, one race category isn't enough. *New York Times.* Accessed November 7, 2017 at http://www.nytimes.com/2001/03/13/national/13CENS.html?module=Search&mabReward=relbias%3As%2C{%222%22%3A%22RI%3A13%22}.

Schroedel, J., Frisch, S., August, R., Kalogris, C., & Perkins, A. (1994). The invisible minority: Asian-American police officers. *State & Local Government Review, 26,* 173–180.

Sharp, C., & Budd, T. (2005). *Minority ethnic groups and crime: Findings from the offending crime and justice survey 2003.* Home Office online report. Accessed November 7, 2017 at http://library.npia.police.uk/docs/hordsolr/rdsolr3305.pdf.

Skogan, W. (2009). Policing immigrant communities in the United States. *Sociology of Crime, Law and Deviance, 13,* 189–203.

Song, J. (1992). Attitudes of Chinese immigrants and Vietnamese refugees toward law enforcement in the United States. *Justice Quarterly, 9,* 703–719.

Song, J., & Hurysz, L. (1995). Victimization patterns of Asian gangs in the United States. *Journal of Gang Research, 3,* 41–49.

Stewart, J. (2001, January 25). Lest hate victim be forgotten: Joseph Ileto's family felt his death at the racist's hand was being ignored. *Los Angeles Times,* p. A1.

Sun, I., & Wu, Y. (2010). Chinese policing in a time of transition, 1978–2008. *Journal of Contemporary Criminal Justice, 26,* 20–35.

Sun, L. (1997, September 9). Anti-Asian American incidents rising, civil rights groups say. *The Washington Post,* p. A2.

Takaki, R. (1998). *Strangers from a different shore: A history of Asian Americans.* New York, NY: Back Bay Books/Little, Brown, and Company.

Terrazas, A., & Batalova, J. (2010). *Chinese immigrants in the United States.* Migration Policy Institute. Accessed November 7, 2017 at http://www.migrationinformation.org/USFocus/display.cfm?ID=781.

Thurman, Q., & Reisig, M. (1996). Community-oriented research in an era of community-oriented policing. *American Behavioral Scientist, 39,* 570–586.

Tichenor, D. (2002). *Dividing lines: The politics of immigration control in America.* Princeton Studies in American Politics. Princeton, NJ: Princeton University Press.

Toro-Morn, M., & Alicea, M. (Eds.). (2004). *Migration and immigration: A global view.* West Pork, CT: Greenwood Press.

Torres, S., & Vogel, R. (2001). Pre and post-test differences between Vietnamese and Latino residents involved in a community policing experiment: Reducing fear of crime and improving attitudes toward the police. *Policing: An International Journal of Police Strategies and Management, 24,* 40–55.

Tuan, M. (2003). *Forever foreigners or honorary Whites? The Asian ethnic experience today.* New Brunswick, NJ: Rutgers University Press.

Turner, K., Feinerman, J., & Guy, K. (Eds.). (2000). *The limits of the rule of law in China.* Seattle, WA: University of Washington Press.

Tyler, T. (1990). *Why people obey the law.* New Haven, CT: Yale University Press.

USA Today. (2005, November 13). *Asian youth persistently harassed by U.S. peers.* Accessed November 7, 2017 at http://usatoday30.usatoday.com/news/nation/2005-11-13-asian-teens-bullied_x.htm.

Uhlaner, C. (1991). Perceived discrimination and prejudice and the coalition prospects of Blacks, Latinos, and Asian Americans. In B. Jackson & M. Preston (Eds.), *Racial and ethnic politics in California* (pp. 339–396). Berkeley, CA: Institute for Governmental Studies.

U.S. Bureau of the Census. (2011). *The American community survey*. Accessed July 4, 2016 at http://factfinder2.census.gov/faces/tableservices/jsf/pages/productview.xhtml?src=bkmk.

Weitzer, R., & Tuch, S. (2005). Determinants of public satisfaction with the police. *Police Quarterly, 8,* 279–297.

Weitzer, R., & Tuch, S. (2006). *Race and policing in America: Conflict and reform*. New York: Cambridge University Press.

Wilson, D. (2001). *Kentucky vehicle stops database: 2001 report*. Accessed July 4, 2017 at http://justice.ky.gov/NR/rdonlyres/15878C81-10EF-443A-B3C3-FD386219B5A1/203507/StatewideRacialProfilingReport2001.pdf.

Wong, M. (2005). Chinese Americans. In P. Min (Ed.), *Asian Americans: Contemporary trends and issues* (pp. 110–145). Thousand Oaks, CA: Sage.

Wortley, S. (1996). Justice for all? Race and perceptions of bias in the Ontario criminal justice system: A Toronto study. *Canadian Journal of Criminology, 38,* 439–467.

Wortley, S., & Owusu-Bempah, A. (2009). Unequal before the law: Immigrant and racial minority perception of the Canadian criminal justice system. *International Migration and Integration, 10,* 447–473.

Wu, Y. (2009). *Race/ethnicity and Chinese immigrants/Americans' perceptions of the police*. Unpublished doctoral dissertation, University of Delaware.

Wu, Y. (2014). Race/ethnicity and perceptions of the police: A comparison of White, Black, Asian, and Hispanic Americans. *Policing & Society, 24,* 135–157.

Wu, Y., Smith, B., & Sun, I. (2013). Race/ethnicity and perceptions of police bias: The case of Chinese immigrants. *Journal of Ethnicity in Criminal Justice, 11,* 71–92.

Wu, Y., Sun, I., & Smith, B. (2011). Race, immigration and policing: Chinese immigrants' satisfaction with police. *Justice Quarterly, 28,* 745–774.

Wu, Y., Sun, I., & Triplett, R. (2009). Race, class or neighborhood context: Which matters more in measuring satisfaction with police. *Justice Quarterly, 26,* 125–156.

Wu, Y., Triplett, R., & Sun, I. (2012). Chinese immigrants' contact with police. *Policing: An International Journal of Police Strategies and Management, 35,* 741–760.

Yen, R. (2000). Racial stereotyping of Asians and Asian Americans and its effect on criminal justice: A reflection on the Wayne Lo case. *Asian Law Journal, 7,* 1–28.

Court Cases

State v. Simon, 231 Kan. 572 (1982).

6

From Invisibility to Unwanted Spotlight: Arab Americans' Perceptions of the Police

Neither White nor Black, Arab Americans are another ethnic group that has received extremely limited attention among crime and justice researchers. For a rather long time, Arab Americans had remained largely invisible to both the law enforcement and research communities. The invisible status of Arab Americans, however, changed dramatically after 2001 when the 9/11 terrorist attacks placed Arab Americans in the cross hares of America's socio-political concerns, and likewise on the radar screen of the nation's law enforcement agencies. Arab Americans and immigrants deserve special research attention at this time, also as the U.S. is led by a president who has openly demonized the religion of Islam and characterized Muslims as the nation's problem (Johnson & Hauslohner, 2017, May 20). Islamophobia threatens the stability of American society, and has serious potential to damage Arab American communities, posing challenges for maintaining inter-group harmony across racial/ethnic groups, as well as between ethnic groups and law enforcement communities.

This chapter summarizes the existing limited but growing literature on Arab Americans' perceptions of the police in the U.S., and equally importantly discusses police-Arab American community relations in

© The Author(s) 2018
I. Y. Sun and Y. Wu, *Race, Immigration, and Social Control,*
Palgrave Studies in Race, Ethnicity, Indigeneity and Criminal Justice,
https://doi.org/10.1057/978-1-349-95807-8_6

their broader historical, political, cultural and social context. Some of the discussion set forth in this chapter also applies to Muslim and South Asian American populations, inasmuch as ethnicity, religion, and place of origin often intersect with one another in shaping people's experience with and perceptions of crime and justice, including in the post-9/11 era (Cainkar, 2009; Detroit Arab American Study Team, 2009).

Arab Americans and Their Communities

Similar to the definitions of Latino and Chinese Americans in this book, the term Arab Americans in this chapter refers to individuals who have an Arab ethnic, cultural and linguistic heritage or identity and who self-identify as Arab. Included in this group are both Arab Americans who were born in the U.S., and immigrants who were born in an Arabic-speaking country and subsequently migrated to the U.S. There are currently twenty-two Arab-speaking countries, and they are concentrated in Southwestern Asia and North Africa. Arab Americans, thusly, may have ancestries of Egyptians, Sudanese, Somali, Libyan, Tunisian, Algerian, Comoro, Djibouti, Moroccan, Mauritanian, Syrian, Jordanian, Palestinian, Lebanese, Iraqi, Saudi Arabian, Yemenite, Kuwaiti, Qatari, Omani, Bahraini, or United Arab Emirates. Quite clearly, Arab Americans are a heterogeneous group of peoples. They have different physical appearances, pursue distinct lifestyles, vary in their religious affiliations, occupy diverse immigrant statuses, and reflect differing patterns and levels of assimilation (Henderson, Ortiz, Sugie, & Miller, 2006; Naber, 2000).

Despite such pronounced diversity, Arab Americans are customarily viewed as a distinct ethnic group by both governmental officials and scholars, given their common historical experience, unity of language, and some shared social customs. The ethnic identity of Arab immigrants overall is strong, with more within group homogeneity observed than among other groups such as Hispanics. This distinction is due in good measure to differences in the homogeneity versus heterogeneity of religious beliefs among Arab immigrants and other immigrant groups (Aly & Ragan, 2010).

It should be noted that the term "Arab American" does not describe a racial identity. The U.S. Census demographic classification system, for example, classifies Arab Americans collectively as Whites or Caucasians. This is because in the early 1900s, for the purpose of citizenship and associated rights, Arab Americans fought for the racial classification of "White," and were eventually defined as White by law since 1944. However, in the 1980s and 1990s, many Arab Americans began to advocate for changing identity markers. Some do not pass phenotypically as Whites (e.g., darker skin), while others do not feel White in American society, and prefer a "non-white" or "people of color" identity (Naber, 2000). Still others choose both ethnic (i.e., Arabs) and White identities simultaneously (Ajrouch & Jamal, 2007). This new trend of growing embracement of a pan-ethnic "Arab American" label is related to "the rise of multiculturalism and ethnic pride, combined with influxes of new, more diverse immigrants" from the Arab world since the 1980s (Kayyali, 2013, p. 1299). Recognizing this trend of identity shift, the U.S. Bureau of the Census has proposed a standalone "Middle Eastern or North African" ("MENA") box for the 2020 census. This change, if implemented, offers Arab Americans the opportunity to identify as MENA, and non-White (Beydoun, 2016).

Regarding immigration background, Arab Americans have an extensive history in the U.S. The first wave of Arab immigrants arrived between the 1870s and the 1920s, mainly from what are today Lebanon and Syria. Early immigrants were primarily Christians and endured a great deal of pressure to assimilate into the American mainstream (Sandoval & Jendrysik, 1993). The social status of Arab Americans back then was described as largely similar to that of Whites, or more exactly, marginal Whites (Cainkar, 2005). The second noteworthy wave of Arab immigration began after World War II, and the third wave began after the 1967 Mid-East War; both subsequent waves were noticeably distinct from the first wave. The majority of the second- and third-wave immigrants were Muslims from a greater number of Arab countries and they tended to possess higher levels of education and more higher-level job skills (Sandoval & Jendrksik, 1993). The experiences of these second and third waves of Arab immigrants, however, were often less than optimal; despite their higher levels of education and broader range of skills many experienced subordinate social status resulting from negative stereotyping and prejudice, exclusion from civil and political affairs, and mass media representations of them as worthy of suspicion (Cainkar, 2005). As aforementioned, officially they were classified as White, yet they were viewed by many of the majority White population as "non-Whites," and in a number of ways they were indeed experientially non-White, leading a large portion of the Arab American group to adopt a "people of color" identity (Cainkar, 2005).

Today, according to the 2011 American Community Survey (U.S. Bureau of the Census, 2011), there were close to 1.8 million Arab Americans living in the U.S. This figure constitutes an approximate increase of 47% in population from 2000. Other estimates of the Arab population suggest that an even higher number of Arab Americans are residing in the U.S. For example, according to the Arab American Institute (2012), the population of Arab Americans has more than doubled since the Census first measured ethnic origins in 1980, and is now closer to 3.7 million. Among Arab Americans, over 80% are U.S. citizens, with 63% being born in this country (Brittingham & de la Cruz, 2005). It is estimated that 98% of Arab Americans speak English (El-Badry & Swanson, 2007). In terms of geography, Arab Americans live in all 50 U.S. states, but fully one third of the total live in the three states of California, New York, and Michigan. About 94% of Arab Americans live in metropolitan areas, with Los Angeles, Detroit, New York/NJ, Chicago and Washington, DC being the top five metropolitan areas of Arab American concentration. With respect to religious belief and affiliation, about two-thirds of Arab Americans are Christian, and the rest mainly Muslim (Henderson et al., 2006).

Arab Americans and Law Enforcement

Although Arab Americans share many features common to the experiences of people of color, for most of their 100-plus year history in the U.S. they remained largely invisible as compared to other minorities such as Blacks, Latinos and Asians. Empirical research on Arab Americans' experience with crime and criminal justice is almost non-existent before 2001, and innovative and successful community policing initiatives often did not reach out to Arab and/or Muslim American communities. In Chicago, for instance, the city's much acclaimed community policing initiative was largely absent in Muslim, Arab, or Sikh American communities pre-9/11. This absence of concerted effort likely can be attributed in most part to the relatively low rates of violent crime occurring within these communities (Ramirez, O'Connell, & Zafar, 2005).

This state of virtual invisibility, however, changed dramatically after 9/11. The terrorist attacks significantly transformed popular discourse regarding Arab and Muslim Americans, placing them in the spotlight of the War on Terror. Arab and Muslim communities across the country were approached by a number of government agencies, educational institutions, and non-profit organizations for engagement in various forms of diversity initiatives (Naber, 2008). This unsolicited attention has led some scholars to characterize Arab Americans as a group that has "evolved from invisible to glaringly conspicuous" (Salaita, 2005, p. 149).

Law enforcement agencies, including local police departments, are now faced with new and powerful pressures to act effectively, in some circumstances aggressively, in the country's War on Terror environment (Lyons, 2002). Federal funding through the Department of Homeland Security has provided state and local agencies, who are now viewed as the primary responders of potential attacks, monetary support for equipment, training, and mock exercises to increase their readiness for major emergencies arising from terrorism (Friedmann & Cannon, 2007). Intelligence-led policing has gained considerable momentum among the nation's police administrators, with different levels of law enforcement agencies prompted to share and manage information regarding risks, vulnerabilities, and incidents related to domestic terrorism, and to expand the capacity of the local police to fight both traditional crime and terrorism (O'Hanlon, 2006; Thacher, 2005).

The events of 9/11 have served to draw considerable law enforcement attention to Arab American communities, oftentimes complicating police-community relations a great deal. On the one hand, law enforcement intelligence gathering and immigration law enforcement in the homeland security context can greatly damage police-Arab American community relations. Shortly after the orchestrated attacks of

9/11, the FBI and many local law enforcement authorities questioned and arrested hundreds of Arab men, mainly for expired visitor or student visas (Bryan, 2005). As previously mentioned, upon the order of Attorney General Ashcroft, the FBI interviewed thousands of Arab and/ or Muslim men who were in the country on temporary visas. Many questions asked were very obtrusive, casting wide doubt on the allegedly voluntary nature of these interviews. Enhanced police surveillance on Arab Americans and their communities heightens the likelihood of them experiencing unfairness, prejudice, and outright hostility in many areas of the country. In addition, not only in the U.S., but also in the United Kingdom and in Australia, studies indicate that there is widespread resentment against counter-terrorism efforts because they are often seen as arbitrarily and disproportionately targeting the minority groups due to their ethnic identity or Islamic faith (Nguyen, 2005; Pickering, McCulloch, & Wright-Neville, 2008; Poynting & Noble, 2004; Rice & Parkin, 2010; Spalek & Imtoual, 2007; Sun, Wu, & Poteyeva, 2011). Muslim Arab Americans, in particular, were more likely than their Christian counterparts to experience discrimination and feel vulnerable and disrespected after the 9/11 (Howell & Jamal, 2009a; Read, 2008).

On the other hand, Arab and/or Muslim Americans, whose sense of personal safety and security was shaken after 9/11, are in dire need of police attention and protection. Arab, South Asian, and Muslim communities commonly feel that they are victims of negative reprisals in the forms of hate crimes, defamatory speech, political backlash, and job discrimination (Cainkar, 2004). Indeed, within one month of 9/11, 45% of Arab Americans reported that someone they knew of Arab ethnicity had experienced discrimination (Zogby, 2001). Within nine weeks of 9/11, there were at least 700 incidents of violence against Arab Americans and anti-Muslim hate crime increased 1600% compared to the previous year (Disha, Cavendish, & King, 2011). Even in Dearborn, Michigan, widely considered to represent the capital of Arab American culture, Arab American neighborhoods were depicted as "ghettos" and "enclaves," and Arab Americans were addressed as "you people" by their non-Arab neighbors (Howell & Shryock, 2003). About 15% of Arab Americans in the Detroit suburban area reported having a negative experience after the 9/11 attacks, involving primarily verbal insults and threats (Howell & Jamal, 2009b). In New Jersey, Jersey City was labeled as a "Terror Town" where dozens of Arab homes and businesses were raided and several local mosques were surveyed (Bryan, 2005). Muslim women in the city endured terrifying ordeals, ranging from children and teenagers throwing rocks and beer cans at them to teenagers punching them "in the face while attempting to rip off their clothes and tear their veils" (Bryan, 2005, p. 143). Victimization among Arab Americans is likely to be underreported as victims feared making any waves or being labeled as trouble-makers (Bryan, 2005). One study reported that Arab community leaders expressed higher levels of perceived hate crime than did local police officers and FBI agents (Hendricks, Oritz, Sugie, & Miller, 2007).

Thus in the post-9/11 era, Arab Americans may have reason to both fear and embrace the police. Their fear intensifies when the police assist in the federal government's counterterrorism policies and efforts, including immigration law enforcement, use of racial and ethnic profiling, employing detentions and deportations, and instituting special registration requirements. However, their need for police protection becomes urgent in areas where hate crimes and violence against Arabs and/or Muslims occur. Correspondingly, the police both tightly monitor this population while at the same time asking it for support in the form of inside intelligence. The counterterrorism effort of the federal government requires the local police in many of the nation's major cities to increase surveillance on Arab community members, while at the same time their efforts to promote community policing impel them to endeavor to build support and willingly cooperation among minority community members, including Arab and Muslim minority communities. All of these pressing but conflicting goals greatly complicate police-Arab community relationships after the events of 9/11.

Arab American Perceptions of the Police

The increased visibility of Arab Americans after 9/11 has promoted some scholarly work on issues of crime and justice for this population; however, this body of research remains limited. For example, literature on victimization and perceptions of crime among Arab Americans concentrates nearly exclusively on hate crimes and intimate partner violence, with a wide range of other types of crime and victimization experiences being neglected and consequently remaining largely unknown (Wu, Klahm, & Atoui, 2016). In regard to Arab Americans' perceptions of the police, there are fewer than a handful of studies to date (Henderson et al., 2006; Klahm & Wu, 2015; Sun & Wu, 2015; Thacher, 2005).

Fortunately, Thacher (2005) conducted a case study on the role of local police departments in homeland security, providing some informative material on police-Arab community relations in Dearborn, Michigan both prior to and after the 9/11 terrorist attacks. The researcher reported that the relationship between Dearborn's Arab community and the local police department was strained in the early 1990s, primarily because of the presence of an openly segregationist mayor. The type of political leadership led to frequent police harassment of Arab American residents and businessmen, the commonplace bullying of Arab American students in schools, and numerous lawsuits filed by Arab American police officers against the department for tolerating a hostile work environment. The police-community relationship has improved, starting in the mid-1990s with the hiring of more Arab American officers, collaborative work with community event organizers, and the establishment of a new police substation in the predominantly Arab area of the city (Thacher, 2005). In 2000, community leaders and local, state and federal law enforcement agencies formed an organization called Advocates and Leaders for Police and Community Trust (ALPACT) to work on issues such as racial profiling that had high potential of damaging police-community relations (Ramirez, O'Connell, & Zafar, 2004). In 2008, Dearborn had its first Arab American police chief (*The Arab American News*, 2008).

City officials' efforts to improve police-community relations, including community policing initiatives had apparently paid off since most Dearborn Arab American residents had come to have trust in their police by the turn of the twenty-first century (Thacher, 2005). Very importantly, the enhanced trust built between Arab Americans and local police had helped minimize the potential conflicts between the two groups after the 9/11 attacks, and prevented serious damage to police legitimacy in that city. The police department quickly beefed up its protection of and patrolling around Arab institutions and neighborhoods after 9/11 in response to Arab residents' concerns about the danger of retaliation and hate crimes (Ramirez et al., 2004). The city government and police department handled the Justice Department's request to interview recent immigrants most cautiously, agreeing to assist federal agents in locating the interviewees, and in some cases serving as translators but declining to conduct the interview themselves (Thacher, 2005).

Thacher's (2005) study was qualitative in nature, while three other studies conducted during this period were quantitative analysis. Also relying on data from the Detroit metropolitan area, Sun and Wu (2015) analyzed the level and correlates of Arab Americans' confidence in the police. The data they used came from the project *Detroit Arab American Study* (DAAS), which included a large sample of almost 1000 adults of Arabic or Chaldean descent. Using probability sampling methods, data were gathered via face-to-face interviews in 2003 by trained researchers from the University of Michigan. The researchers found that the majority of Arab Americans surveyed expressed favorable opinions on their local police. Specifically, over 85% of the survey participants said they had "a great deal" or "a lot" of confidence in local police, with only 11.1 and 3.4% reporting that they had "not very much" or "none at all" confidence in local police, respectively. These survey results were comparable with 2003 U.S. national data showing that approximately 90% of Americans reported having a great deal or some confidence in the police at that time (The Sourcebook of Criminal Justice Statistics, 2003).

It should be noted, however, that the same Arab American survey participants who took part in the Detroit metropolitan area study did not express positive views on counter-terrorism measures. Sun et al. (2011) found that only a modest number of Arab Americans endorsed aggressive law enforcement measures against the general public, and a much smaller number supported counterterrorism measures that targeted Arab Americans exclusively. Specifically, only slightly over half of the respondents supported the idea of increasing surveillance of U.S. citizens by the government as a way to deter and/or prevent terrorist acts. A much lower proportion of the respondents (23%) supported giving the police power to stop and search anyone at random. About one in five of the respondents (19%) favored detaining some suspicious individuals even in absence of sufficient evidence to prosecute them in the courts. These results suggest that the level of public support decreases with the increase in the aggressiveness of law enforcement measures and the potential of violations of individual liberties and rights. When it comes to targeting Arab Americans in specific, only 15% of the respondents said they would support increasing surveillance of Arab Americans by the government. Merely 7% were in favor of giving the police the power to randomly stop and search anyone who appeared to be Arab or Muslim, and 12% upheld the idea that police could detain more suspicious Arabs and/or Muslims even if there was no sufficient evidence to prosecute them in the courts.

Eleven years after the DAAS project, in a project entitled *Arab Americans' Victimization and Fear of Crime in Metro-Detroit* (AAVFC), one of the authors of this book again collected survey interview data within the Detroit metropolitan area, using probability sampling methods. Ten trained bilingual interviewers from Wayne State University were sent to selected households in Dearborn and Dearborn Heights to conduct the face-to-face interviews. The study found that Arab-Americans continued to express favorable ratings of their local police. When asked the same question about their level of confidence in police as were asked in the DAAS project years earlier, 40.6% of the survey participants reported "a great deal" and 36.2% reported "a lot" of confidence. As shown in Fig. 6.1, the 2003 and 2014 data were virtually identical in the first ("a great deal") and last ("none at all") response categories. Compared to the 2003 results, the 2014 data showed a lower percentage in the "a lot" category (45.4% v. 36.2%) and a higher percentage in the "not much" category (11.1% v. 19.8%). However, these differences were not statistically significant, indicating that Arab Americans' confidence in their local police had remained largely unchanged over the course of the intervening decade in metro-Detroit.

Based on the AAFVC data, Klahm and Wu (2015), further, compared the perceptions of the police held by Arab and non-Arab Americans; their data consisted of 211 Arab American residents and

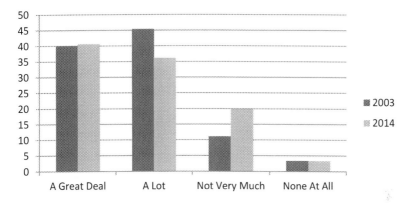

Fig. 6.1 Arab Americans confidence in police (*Source* Authors' calculation)

203 non-Arab American residents. They reported that Arab and non-Arab respondents did not differ significantly in their perceptions of how the local police treat people, their ratings of the effectiveness of the police, or their willingness to cooperate with the police, net of a range of control variables such as demographic characteristics, victimization experience, fear of crime, media exposure to police, and neighborhood conditions. So, more than a decade after 9/11 Arab American residents in the Detroit metropolitan area were not more likely than their non-Arab American counterparts to feel they are being treated poorly by the police. Not only were no significant differences found in the respondents' perceptions of police equality and effectiveness based on ethnicity, but Arab and non-Arab respondents indicated a similar willingness to assist the police in the pursuit of their crime fighting efforts.

All these positive results appear to paint a very positive picture of Arab Americans' perceptions of the police in the metro-Detroit area. These findings, however, may be context-specific and may not apply to other areas in the U.S. As widely known, metro-Detroit has one of the largest, oldest, most concentrated, and best-known Arab expatriate populations in the world, hosting more than 400,000 Arab Americans. Both the DAAS and the AAVFC studies included data from the Cities of Dearborn and Dearborn Heights in Wayne County (part of metro-Detroit). Dearborn, a southwest suburb of Detroit with a total area of 24.5 square miles, is known as the center of Arab-America because over 40% of the city's 98,153 residents are of Arab ancestry, making Middle-Eastern ancestries the largest ethnic group in the area (U.S. Bureau of the Census, 2010). Dearborn Heights, adjacent to Dearborn, has a total area of 11.75 square miles, and approximately 10% of the city's 57,774 residents are of Arab Ancestry (U.S. Bureau of the Census, 2010).

The heavy concentration of Arab Americans in these areas may contribute to their positive views on the police, most likely through three possible mechanisms. First, the local Arab communities are highly institutionalized with effective community organizations, enjoy considerable political prominence, and have a good deal of general support from prosperous benefactors. Dearborn, for example, is home to the Arab American National Museum, a city council primarily governed by Arab American representatives, a police force led by an Arab American chief, and countless shops and eateries featuring Arabic influence. Several big box stores, such as Home Depot and Meijer post signs in English and standard Arabic, indicating that Arab Americans are a significant and important part of the community. Taken together, these elements may create a cultural synchronicity that leads residents to be less fearful of police bias and more confident in the receipt of police protection when needed.

Second, it is possible that metro-Detroit Arab Americans' historical experiences of suspicion (e.g., being watched, doubted, and asked to prove their loyalties) and subsequent inclusion (i.e., being incorporated, recognized, and rewarded for participation in the American mainstream system) have made them resilient and adaptive, and subsequently they fared much better than those in other cities after the 9/11 attacks (Shryock & Lin, 2009). Santoro and Azab (2015) reported that large numbers of Arab American protests and Arab American protests targeting repression occurred in metro-Detroit 1999–2010, excluding protest directed at international concerns such as the Iraqi war and domestic issues unrelated to state surveillance/harassment or private citizen assaults. They revealed the active mobilization and justice-seeking of Arab Americans in reaction to crises, and reflect the collective identity and power that Arab metro-Detroiters have demonstrated over the course of a decade. Besides protests, local Arab Americans also adapt to anti-Arab backlash periods by displays of hyper patriotism. It is widely observed that it is possible to identify Arab American drivers by their choice of Ford pick-up trucks most likely festooned by American flags. Even three years after 9/11, Arab neighborhoods were notable for the many American flags hanging from the front porches of the houses there (Staeheli & Nagel, 2008).

Third, local police departments in metro-Detroit have made great sustained efforts to establish solid rapport with their Arab American communities after 9/11. As noted, the police cautiously decided to avoid active involvement in federal investigation of terrorists, and performed proactive patrol strategies to protect Arab persons and their neighborhoods in the aftermath of the 9/11 attacks (Sun & Wu, 2015). These progressive measures can all help in maintaining positive regard for police among Arab Americans.

While all these ideas are certainly reasonable explanations for contextualizing the findings on positive attitudes toward the police among metro-Detroit's Arab Americans, they have yet to be validated empirically. There is no study that compares and contrasts Arab Americans' perceptions of the police in metro-Detroit with other areas. To date, only one study has featured multiple research sites. Henderson et al. (2006), based on a combination of telephone interviews, in-person interviews, and focus group interview sessions with community leaders, police personnel, and FBI agents in sixteen jurisdictions, examined the relationship between law enforcement and the Arab American community in the U.S. after 9/11. All sixteen of the locations examined were home to a substantial, geographically highly concentrated Arab-American community. It was found that Arab Americans rated their local police positively even in jurisdictions where there was little interaction between the two. Arab Americans' perceptions of federal law enforcement, however, were less favorable. The central role that federal agencies have played in fighting terrorism and enforcing immigration laws may contribute to this higher level of fear and suspicion of federal law enforcement (Henderson et al., 2006). Additionally, although Arab Americans expressed a fair degree of trust and good will toward local police in the aftermath of 9/11, they were reportedly more fearful of the police and less trustful of law enforcement overall, particularly on issues of immigration enforcement, surveillance, and racial profiling (Henderson et al., 2006).

As little as we know about Arab Americans' levels of confidence in the police, we know even less about factors that can affect Arab Americans' perceptions of the police. Four groups of predictors have been investigated in the limited research available. The first group consists of individual demographic characteristics. Contrary to popular belief, Arab Americans' immigrant status, ethnicity, and religious belief were not found to affect their confidence in the police to any significant degree. The 2003 DAAS study revealed that foreign- and U.S.-born, White and non-White, and Muslim and non-Muslim Arab respondents did not vary significantly in their confidence in the police (Sun & Wu, 2015). Exceptionally, there is rather good evidence showing that education level and age shaped Arab Americans' perceptions of the police to a noteworthy extent. Sun and Wu (2015) found that Arab American respondents who had a high school diploma or lower educational attainment were more likely to report confidence in the local police. Klahm and Wu (2015) revealed that older Arab respondents were more likely to believe the police treat people equally and to be willing to cooperate with the police, similar to what has been found among the general U.S. population (Brown & Benedict, 2002).

The second group of predictors includes social attitudes and trust. Sun and Wu (2015) reported that Arab Americans who have greater confidence in the U.S. legal system, more respect for authority, and trust in their neighbors were more likely to report confidence in the local police. The third group of predictors points to social ties and power. Jamal (2005) showed that Arab Muslims who lacked organizational ties had lower levels of ethnic solidarity, leading to a lower tendency to interpret police mistreatment of fellow Arab Muslims as a form of injustice. The last group of predictors taps into Arab Americans' direct experience with crime and justice. Klahm and Wu (2015) reported that being a victim of crime during the past three years was significantly related to less favorable evaluations of police equal treatment and effectiveness among Arab Americans. Personal negative experience after 9/11, however, was not found to link to Arab Americans' overall confidence in the police (Sun & Wu, 2015).

Regarding factors that influence Arab Americans' willingness to cooperate with the police, both procedural justice and effectiveness have received some empirical support. Klahm and Wu (2015) found that perceptions of police effectiveness, rather than police equal treatment, affected Arab Americans' willingness to cooperate with the police in the areas of reporting crime, providing information, and being willing to serve as a witness in courts in the metro-Detroit area. In contrast, based on data from two targeted samples of Muslim Americans in the New York City in 2009 and 2010, Tyler, Schulhofer, and Huq (2011) found that procedural justice was a critical determinant of police legitimacy and willingness to cooperate. Procedural justice was measured by a combination of fairness of procedure that the police use to handle problems and how the police treat people. Tyler and his colleagues found procedural justice to be a significant predictor of perceived police legitimacy and cooperation in policing efforts against both common crime and terrorism, among **both** Muslims and non-Muslims. Finally, in a study conducted in Australia, willingness to cooperate with the police in typical crime control activities was determined predominantly by judgments of police legitimacy among Arabic-speaking people (Cherney & Murphy, 2013).

Summary

The stability of high levels of confidence in the local police among Arab Americans as suggested by the existing preliminary evidences is encouraging. They may reflect the strong resilience of Arab Americans, particularly those residing in long-term ethnic-concentrated areas, in fighting anti-immigration backlash and leading a positive life, as well as the due attention and protection that local police departments render to ethnic communities.

Despite preliminary, data suggest that factors that affect Arab Americans' perception of the police are not so distinct from those that affect the rest of American population. Age, education, victimization, social trust, and traditional values are some example variables that shape Arab American confidence in the police. Police performances in both effective crime control and procedurally just treatment are also key promoters of Arab American perceptions of police legitimacy and willingness to cooperate with the police. That being said, more research is in a dire need to unpack the sequence of events that link Arab ethnicity and experience to perceptions, and identify the relationship between group dynamic, ethnic culture, and collective perception.

References

Ajrouch, K., & Jamal, A. (2007). Assimilating to a white identity: The case of Arab Americans. *International Migration Review, 41,* 860–879.

Aly, A., & Ragan, J. (2010). Arab immigrants in the United States: How and why do returns to education vary by country? *Journal of Population Economics, 23,* 519–538.

Arab American Institute. (2012). *Demographics.* Accessed March 20, 2013 at http://aai.3cdn.net/2b24e6a8711d521148_5ym6iv4b5.pdf.

Beydoun, K. (2016). Boxed in: Reclassification of Arab Americans on the U.S. census as progress or peril? *Loyola University Chicago Law Journal, 47,* 693–759.

Brittingham, A., & de la Cruz, P. (2005). *We the people of Arab ancestry in the United States* (Census 2000 special reports). Accessed January 1, 2015 at https://www.census.gov/prod/2005pubs/censr-21.pdf.

Brown, B., & Benedict, W. (2002). Perceptions of the police: Past findings, methodological issues, conceptual issues and policy implications. *Policing: An International Journal of Police Strategies and Management, 25,* 543–580.

Bryan, J. (2005). Constructing "the true Islam" in hostile times: The impact of 9/11 on Arab Muslims in Jersey City. In N. Foner (Ed.), *Wounded city: The social impact of 9/11* (pp. 133–159). New York: Russell Sage Foundation.

Cainkar, L. (2004). The impact of the September 11 attacks on Arab and Muslim communities in the United States. In J. Tirman (Ed.), *The maze of fear: Security and migration after 9/11* (pp. 215–240). New York, NY: The New Press.

Cainkar, L. (2005). Space and place in the Metropolis: Arabs and Muslims seeking safety. *City and Society, 17,* 181–209.

Cainkar, L. (2009). *Homeland insecurity: The Arab American and Muslim American experience after 9/11.* New York: Russell Sage Foundation.

Cherney, A., & Murphy, K. (2013). Policing terrorism with procedural justice: The role of police legitimacy and law legitimacy. *Australian & New Zealand Journal of Criminology, 46,* 403–421.

Detroit Arab American Study Team. (2009). *Citizenship and crisis: Arab Detroit after 9/11.* New York: Russell Sage Foundation.

Disha, I., Cavendish, J., & King, R. (2011). Historical events and spaces of hate. *Social Problems, 58,* 21–46.

El-Badry, S., & Swanson, D. (2007). Providing census tabulations to government security agencies in the United States: The case of Arab Americans. *Government Information Quarterly, 24,* 470–487.

Friedmann, R., & Cannon, W. (2007). Homeland security and community policing: Competing or complementing public safety policies. *Journal of Homeland Security and Emergency Management, 4,* 1372–1391.

Henderson, N., Ortiz, C., Sugie, N., & Miller, J. (2006). *Law enforcement and Arab American community relations after September 11, 2001: Engagement in a time of uncertainty.* New York: Vera Institute of Justice.

Hendricks, N., Oritz, C., Sugie, N., & Miller, J. (2007). Beyond the numbers: Hate crimes and cultural trauma within Arab American immigrant community. *International Review of Victimology, 14,* 95–113.

Howell, S., & Jamal, A. (2009a). Belief and belonging. In Detroit Arab American Study Team (Eds.), *Citizenship and crisis: Arab Detroit after 9/11* (pp. 103–134). New York: Russell Sage Foundation.

Howell, S., & Jamal, A. (2009b). The aftermath of the 9/11 attacks. In Detroit Arab American Study Team (Eds.), *Citizenship and crisis: Arab Detroit after 9/11* (pp. 69–100). New York: Russell Sage Foundation.

Howell, S., & Shryock, A. (2003). Cracking down on diaspora: Arab Detroit and America's "war on terror". *Anthropological Quarterly, 76,* 443–462.

Jamal, A. (2005). The political participation and engagement of Muslim Americans: Mosque involvement and group consciousness. *American Politics Research, 33,* 521–544.

Johnson, J., & Hauslohner, A. (2017, May 20). I think Islam hates us: A timeline of Trump's comments about Islam and Muslims. *The Washington Post.* Accessed June 1, 2017 at https://www.washingtonpost.com/news/post-politics/wp/2017/05/20/i-think-islam-hates-us-a-timeline-of-trumps-comments-about-islam-and-muslims/?utm_term=.28b389b23617.

Kayyali, R. (2013). US Census classifications and Arab Americans: Contestations and definitions of identity markers. *Journal of Ethnic and Migration Studies.* Accessed December 30, 2017 at https://doi.org/10.1080/1369183X.2013.778150.

Klahm, C., & Wu, Y. (2015). *Arab Americans' perceptions of the police in two cities.* Paper presented at the annual meeting of the American Society of Criminology, Washington, DC.

Lyons, W. (2002). Partnerships, information, and public safety: Community policing in a time of terror. *Policing: An International Journal of Police Strategies & Management, 25,* 530–542.

Naber, N. (2000). Ambiguous insiders: An investigation of Arab American invisibility. *Ethnic and Racial Studies, 23,* 37–61.

Naber, N. (2008). Arab Americans and U.S. racial formation. In A. Jamal & N. Naber (Eds.), *Race and Arab Americans before and after 9/11: From invisible citizens to visible subjects* (pp. 1–45). Syracuse: Syracuse University Press.

Nguyen, T. (2005). *We are all suspects now: Untold stories from immigrant communities after 9/11.* Boston: Beacon Press.

O'Hanlon, M. (2006). The role of D.O.D. and first responders. In M. d'Arcy, M. O'Hanlon, P. Orszag, J. Shapiro, & J. Steinberg (Eds.), *Protecting the Homeland 2006/2007* (pp. 113–128). Washington, DC: Brookings Institute Press.

Pickering, S., McCulloch, J., & Wright-Neville, D. (2008). Counter-terrorism policing: Towards social cohesion. *Crime, Law & Social Change, 50,* 91–109.

Poynting, S., & Noble, G. (2004). *Living with racism: The experience and reporting by Arab and Muslim Australians of discrimination, abuse and violence since September 11, 2001.* Report to the Human Rights and Equal Opportunity Commission. Sydney: Centre for Cultural Research, University of Western Sydney.

Ramirez, D., O'Connell, S., & Zafar, R. (2004). *Developing partnerships between law enforcement and American Muslim, Arab, and Sikh communities: A promising practices guide.* Boston, MA: Northeastern University.

Ramirez, D., O'Connell, S., & Zafar, R. (2005). *Developing partnerships between law enforcement and American Muslim, Arab, and Sikh communities: The greater Boston experience follow up case study.* Boston: The Partnership for Prevention and Community Safety Initiative. Accessed January 1, 2016 at http://www.spcs.neu.edu/pfp/downloads/Boston_Case_Study.pdf.

Read, J. (2008). Discrimination and identity formation in a post-9/11 era: A comparison of Muslim and Christian Arab Americans. In A. Jamal & N. Naber (Eds.), *Race and Arab Americans before and after 9/11: From invisible citizens to visible subjects* (pp. 305–317). Syracuse, NY: Syracuse University Press.

Rice, S., & Parkin, W. (2010). New avenues for profiling and bias research: The question of Muslim Americans. In S. Rice & M. White (Eds.), *Race, ethnicity and policing: New and essential readings* (pp. 450–467). New York: New York University Press.

Salaita, S. (2005). Ethnic identity and imperative patriotism: Arab Americans before and after 9/11. *College Literature, 32,* 146–168.

Sandoval, J., & Jendrksik, M. (1993). Convergence and divergence in Arab-American public opinion. *International Journal of Public Opinion Research, 5,* 303–314.

Santoro, W., & Azab, M. (2015). Arab American protest in the terror decade: Macro- and micro-level response to post-9/11 repression. *Social Problems, 62,* 219–240.

Shryock, A., & Lin, A. (2009). The limits of citizenship. In Detroit Arab American Study Team (Eds.), *Citizenship and crisis: Arab Detroit after 9/11* (pp. 265–286). New York: Russell Sage Foundation.

Spalek, B., & Intoual, A. (2007). Muslim communities and counter-terror responses: "Hard" approaches to community engagement in the UK and Australia. *Journal of Muslim Minority Affairs, 27,* 185–202.

Staeheli, L., & Nagel, C. (2008). Rethinking security: Perspectives from Arab-American and British Arab activists. *Antipode, 40,* 780–801.

Sun, I., & Wu, Y. (2015). Arab Americans' confidence in police. *Crime & Delinquency, 61,* 483–508.

Sun, I., Wu, Y., & Poteyeva, M. (2011). Arab Americans' support for counter-terrorism measures: The impact of race, ethnicity, and religion. *Studies in Conflict and Terrorism, 34,* 540–555.

Thacher, D. (2005). The local role in homeland security. *Law and Society Review, 39,* 635–676.

The Arab American News. (2008). *Haddad begins job as Dearborn police chief.* Accessed May 24, 2010 at http://www.arabamericannews.com/news/index.php?mod=article&cat=Community&article=1793.

The Sourcebook of Criminal Justice Statistics. (2003). Washington, DC: Bureau of Justice Statistics. Accessed November 7, 2017 at http://www.albany.edu/sourcebook/tost_2.html.

Tyler, T., Schulhofer, S., & Huq, A. (2011). Why does the public cooperate with law enforcement? The influence of the purposes and targets of policing. *Psychology, Public Policy & Law, 17,* 419–450.

U.S. Bureau of the Census. (2010). *2010 ancestry report for Dearborn.* Accessed January 12, 2012 at http://factfinder2.census.gov/faces/tableservices/jsf/pages/productview.xhtml?pid=ACS_10_1YR_DP02&prodType=table.

U.S. Bureau of the Census. (2011). *2011 American community survey 1-year estimates*. Accessed February 27, 2013 at http://factfinder2.census.gov/faces/nav/jsf/pages/searchresults.xhtml?refresh=t.

Wu, Y., Klahm, C., & Atoui, N. (2016). Fear of crime among Arab Americans in a culture of fear. *Ethnic and Racial Studies*. Online first at http://www.tandfonline.com/action/showAxaArticles?journalCode=rers20.

Zogby, J. (2001). *A poll of Arab-Americans since the terrorist attacks on the United States*. Washington, DC: Arab American Institute. Accessed January 1, 2014 at www.aaiusa.org/index_ee.php/reports/arab-american-attitudes-the-september-11-attacks.

7

More Than Blacks and Whites: Theory Development on Immigrant Perceptions of the Police

The previous three chapters have focused on the experience of three minority groups with the police—namely, Latino, Chinese and Arab Americans. Considered individually, each group has unique characteristics; collectively, they share some commonalities as ethnic minorities with large proportions of foreign-born individuals in an increasingly multicultural yet still hierarchical and White-privileged society (Feagin, 2013). This chapter is devoted to the accomplishment of two principal tasks: (1) presenting a review of the empirical evidence reported in systematic research involving the comparison of attitudes toward police across two or more minority groups in the U.S. and (2) proposing a conceptual framework that can help explain immigrant minority attitudes toward the police. While some of the research discussed in this chapter may have been presented earlier in the book, this chapter offers a holistic overview and discussion of that research, zeroing in on the common and group-specific covariates of public perceptions

A revised version of this chapter has appeared in Wu, Y., Sun, I., & Cao, L. (2017). Immigrant perceptions of the police: Theoretical explanations. *International Journal of Police Science and Management, 19*, 171–186.

I. Y. Sun and Y. Wu, *Race, Immigration, and Social Control*,
Palgrave Studies in Race, Ethnicity, Indigeneity and Criminal Justice,
https://doi.org/10.1057/978-1-349-95807-8_7

of the police among U.S. racial and ethnic immigrants. Importantly, this chapter outlines an encompassing theoretical framework that can effectively integrate past research and serve as a springboard for launching future research.

Differential Attitudes Toward Police Across Groups

Studies that are comparative in nature are particularly difficult to conduct, but they have special merits with respect to insight—both substantive and theory-building oriented alike. By comparing and contrasting, researchers can document the uniqueness of a particular group as well as identify social dynamics that are common to different groups. Research into public perceptions of the police that includes two or more minority groups simultaneously remains quite limited. As previously mentioned, the majority of the extant studies pertain to comparisons between Blacks and Hispanics. Most such studies report that Hispanic attitudes toward the police were generally in the "middle ground" between Whites and Blacks, with satisfaction levels lower than those of Whites yet higher than those of Blacks (Buckler & Unnever, 2008; Garcia & Cao, 2005; Lai & Zhao, 2010; Schafer, Huebner, & Bynum, 2003; Schuck & Rosenbaum, 2005; Taylor, Turner, Esbensen, & Winfree, 2001; Walker, 1997; Webb & Marshall, 1995; Weitzer, 2002). This rank ordering of attitudes toward the police would appear to apply to a wide variety of issues, including trust in police, confidence in police performance, satisfaction with officer demeanor, perceptions of police fairness, opinion on racially biased policing, assessment of police corruption, use of excessive force, engagement in verbal abuse and frequent unwarranted stops, and others (Brown & Benedict, 2002; Peck, 2015; Weitzer & Tuch, 2006).

Most studies feature too few Asians, Native Americans, or other minority groups to make separate statistical analysis meaningful. Lumping non-Black, non-Hispanic minority groups into an "others" category makes results extremely difficult to interpret, if not outright impossible. Based on data from in-depth interviews and vignettes among a sample of male juveniles in a minimum security correctional facility, Feinstein (2015) revealed that Native American juveniles were more likely than their White counterparts to believe that people of color did not receive "second chances" from the police as often as Whites do. They likewise tend to believe that the police use unnecessary force against people of color more often than they do against Whites. Taylor et al. (2001), based on student samples drawn in 11 American cities, revealed that American Indian students reported more favorable attitudes toward the police than Blacks, but less favorable attitudes than Whites.

Regarding Asian Americans, while the 11-city student data indicated quite favorable attitudes toward the police among Asian Americans overall (Taylor et al., 2001), Wu (2014) found that Asian American residents in Seattle reported more negative perceptions of police hassling and racial profiling than White residents. Wu (2014) also compared Asian and Hispanic Americans' attitudes toward the police, showing that while the two groups thought similarly with respect to some aspects of police performance, Hispanics held more negative views about police equal treatment than did Asians. Torres and Vogel (2001) compared Vietnamese and Latino perceptions of the police in Garden Grove, CA, discovering more favorable views held by the Vietnamese than the Latino residents. Also using data from California, Song (1992) found that Chinese immigrants expressed significantly greater concerns of police prejudice against minority residents than did Vietnamese refugees in the Los Angeles area.

Albeit limited in scope and number, the extant studies once again highlighted the heterogeneity obtaining among racial/ethnic minority groups regarding attitudes toward the police. Coupled with the substantial evidence presented in previous chapters pertaining to the varied views on the police existing within racial/ethnic groups, it is clear that the matter of public perceptions of the police is very complicated. Attitude formation toward the police would seem to involve interplays of multiple dimensions of race, ethnicity, immigration experience, culture, direct and vicarious experience with police officers, and many others. In view of this seemingly "messy" set of research results, it becomes urgent to strengthen our theorizing effort on the subject. The research which has been carried out over the course of the past two decades on the determinants of immigrants' perceptions of the police can be considered both sparse and largely a-theoretical. Although several theoretically implicated covariates have been investigated in the literature, researchers have not yet proposed a substantive theoretical core that can be applied across immigrant populations. In this chapter, we propose such an integrated conceptual model to explain immigrant minority perceptions of the police.

Integrated Conceptual Model

The conceptual model we propose aims to further our understanding regarding the sociological structure, cultural context, and attitude formation process that contribute to ethnically differentiated views on the police in the U.S. It identifies fundamental dimensions and relationships in attitudes toward the police that possibly cut across group boundaries, showing a certain level of breadth and universal power of prediction. This model, based on a prototype Wu and associates (2011) proposed and tested to a limited extent, makes important extensions to that prototype and derives testable theories that pertain to each major component of the model. Table 7.1 presents the main domains of the model, along with the associated theories and their example variables/indicators.

In a nutshell, this integrated model reflects the view that immigrant attitudes toward the police are subject to two principal sources of influence: *universal factors* that tend to shape all residents' attitudes toward the police, and *group-specific factors* that only apply to foreign-born individuals. Within both universal and immigrant-specific factors, there are four subcategories of demographic, experiential, structural, and attitudinal variables having potential effects on attitudes. Some of these variables are post-arrival variables, meaning that they involve immigrants' lives after their migration experience, whereas others are pre-arrival variables, referring to those experiences and perceptions that occurred before the migration experience. Notably, this model not only incorporates a wide range of variables, but it also classifies and unifies a variety of theoretical perspectives that we will explain one-by-one below.

Table 7.1 An integrated conceptual framework of immigrant perceptions of the police

	Indicators	Theories	Temporal order
Universal factors			
1. Demographic	Race/ethnicity	Group position theory	Post-arrival
		Racial hierarchy theory	
	Social class	Socioeconomic resource thesis	
2. Experiential	Experience with police	Institutional performance theory	Post-arrival
	Experience with crime		
3. Structural	Neighborhood conditions	Social disorganization theory	Post-arrival
	City/region context	Community accountability perspective	
4. Attitudinal	Senses of injustice	Sense of injustice perspective	Post-arrival
		Procedural justice theory	
		Multifaceted discrimination model	
	Group consciousness	Group consciousness theory	
Group-specific factors			
1. Demographic	Foreign-born status	Immigrant paradox thesis	Post-arrival
	Degree of assimilation	Assimilation theory	
2. Experiential	Contact with home country police	Imported socialization theory	Pre-arrival
	Experience with home country crime	Contrast thesis	
	Contact with U.S. immigration officers	Trust-transference hypothesis	
3. Structural	Nature of regime	Critical citizen thesis	Pre-arrival
4. Attitudinal	Authoritarian values	Cultural thesis	Pre-arrival

Universal Variables 1: Demographic

The first category of universal variables consists of individual demographic characteristics. While there are most certainly other significant individual predictors such as age and level of formal education, **race/ethnicity** and **social class** arguably are the most salient and frequently examined predictors of public attitudes toward the police. Three established theories can be used to explain attitudinal variations across race, ethnicity and class—namely, *group position theory*, *racial hierarchy theory*, and *socioeconomic resource theory*.

Group Position Theory

Group position theory, previously introduced in Chapter 2, is perhaps the most often used theoretical perspective in guiding research on public attitudes toward police. Originating from Blumer's (1958) group-position theory of racial prejudice, this theory predicts that a sense of group position in a society determines group sentiments toward social institutions in that society. In line with Blalock's racial threat thesis (1967), this theory suggests that members of the dominant group in a society tend to share a sense of superiority and view members of the subordinate group as both threats to dominant group prerogatives and competitors of limited resources (Bobo & Tuan, 2006). Weitzer and Tuch (2006) applied this theory to explaining public attitudes toward the police, arguing that Whites hold more favorable views of the police because they perceive this social institution as a critical resource to own, and more importantly, as important protectors of their interests and status superiority. The negative stereotyping of racial/ethnic minorities as prone to violence and criminality held by many Whites further adds to White support for aggressive law enforcement against minority Americans and in high minority concentration neighborhoods (Holmes & Smith, 2008). In contrast, the social and political marginality status of ethnic minorities leads to their more negative views on the police, deeming the police as mainly being engaged in controlling minorities and maintaining the social status quo (Wu, Sun, & Triplett, 2009).

While somewhat less applicable, the theory can also help explain the attitudes of minority groups other than Blacks. Latino and Asian Americans, for example, also suffer "out-group stereotyping" from Whites (Bobo & Hutchings, 1996, p. 955), and are often viewed as threats to long-prevailing majority privileges. Partially due to phenotypical differences from the Anglo majority, many Latino and Asian Americans are subjects of the "perpetual foreigner" stereotype, being viewed as ineradicably foreign regardless of their citizenship status or the extent of their acculturation into the American culture (Bender & Braveman, 1995; Xie & Goyette, 2003). This stereotyping brings subsequent nativist arguments advocating limits on the rights of these perpetual "foreigners" (Yakushko, 2009). Correspondingly, the members of these minority groups may view the police more negatively than Whites, believing the police represent the dominant White society and contribute to the existing patterns of racial/ethnic inequality in the society. Although there are a small number of studies comparing attitudes toward the police among Latino, Asian, Black, and/or White Americans (see Peck, 2015 for a review), there has yet to be any research that has specifically compared Latino or Asian immigrant perceptions to those of Black and White Americans.

Racial Hierarchy Theory

The group position theory was originally anchored in a biracial paradigm and did not elaborate on the potential inter-minority variations on attitudes toward the police (Wu, 2014). Comparably, the racial hierarchy theory is perhaps more helpful in explaining attitudinal variations *among* minority groups, including immigrant minority groups. Racial hierarchy theory holds that "groups are defined in relation to one another and treated accordingly, resulting in differentiated group statuses and privileges" (Kim, 2004, p. 997). In this hierarchy, Whites are typically on top, with people of color being arrayed below in relation to Whites and to one another (Twomey, 2001). Regarding attitudes toward the police, different minority groups may have differential levels of alienation from the police, with "members of more recent and voluntarily incorporated minority groups" feeling "less alienation than members of long-term and involuntarily incorporated minority groups" (Bobo, 1999, p. 461). Accordingly, non-Black, non-White minority groups are expected to be located in the middle of the racial hierarchy of the level of satisfaction with the police.

Non-Black minority groups, such as Hispanic and Asian Americans, may encounter similar challenges to those that Black Americans have experienced, such as discrimination in education, housing, health care and employment, and victimization by hate crimes (Pager & Shepherd, 2008). They, meanwhile, differ from Black Americans on many fronts, including their experience with the criminal justice system. For example, Black Americans are much more over-represented in the criminal justice system as both offenders and victims than other groups (Gabbidon & Greene, 2013), increasing their chances of experiencing negative encounters with the police. It is thus reasonable to contend that many immigrant minority groups do not occupy a similarly unique alienated position that Black Americans hold in the U.S.; consequently, they do not have similarly high levels of distrust in the police. Again, no research could be located that has directly compared the perceptions of the police between immigrant groups to those of White and Black (non-immigrant) Americans.

Socioeconomic Resource Thesis

Socioeconomic resource theory emphasizes the role that social class and associated resources play in shaping people's behaviors and attitudes across a broad range of matters affecting social life. It is based on the assumption that individuals in a society "are ranked hierarchically in terms of their economics and social status, affording them different types and amounts of resources" (Berg, 2010, p. 279). This perspective gives prominence to social inequality as a barrier to achieving positive police-community relations, and frames the politically sensitive issue of racial and ethnic differences in primarily socio-economic terms (McAllister & Makkai, 1992).

Though not addressing the issue of police-citizen relations, Wilson (1978), in *The Declining Significance of Race*, argues that although race remains a factor, social class has become more important in determining people's lives and attitudes in the post-Civil Rights era. Wilson's (1978) general assertion that race is declining in significance suggests that Blacks and Whites, especially those growing up in the post-civil rights era, would be similar rather than dissimilar in their attitudes toward the police (Browning & Cao, 1992).

The socioeconomic resource theory would expect that immigrant groups that have on average higher socioeconomic statuses (SES) will have more favorable evaluations of the police than their counterparts with lower average SESs, and within a certain group, those who have more socioeconomic resources will hold more positive views on the police than the less advantaged. This postulation has received some empirical support. For example, Song (1992) compared Chinese immigrants' and Vietnamese refugees' attitudes toward law enforcement. He found that Vietnamese refugees consistently rated problems such as poor communication between police and residents, slow police response to calls, and perceived police prejudice against ethnic immigrants more seriously than did the Chinese. As Vietnamese refugees on average have lower levels of SES compared to Chinese immigrants (Xie & Goyette, 2003), these results seem to provide indirect support for the socioeconomic resource thesis. Within a single immigrant group, the effects of social class on perceptions are more mixed. Pertaining to employment, Wu and colleagues (2011) found that full-time employment reduced Chinese immigrants' satisfaction with police demeanour and integrity. As to educational attainment, two studies found that education was negatively related to immigrants' evaluations of police effectiveness (Chu, Song, & Dombrink, 2005; Davis & Hendricks, 2007), one study revealed positive effects of education on immigrant views on the police (Khondaker, Wu, & Lamber, 2016), while two others found no relationship (Correia, 2010; Wu, Sun, & Smith, 2011). Regarding income, its connection to immigrants' perceptions of the police has yet to be established (Chu et al., 2005; Wu et al., 2011).

Universal Variables 2: Experiential

The next category of universal variables is about individual experience with crime and justice. Two factors, experience with the police and experience with crime, are particularly relevant as the police are commonly viewed as the main governmental agency responsible for crime control, disorder subdual, and fear reduction (Wilson, 1975).

Institutional Performance Theory

Applying institutional performance theory, one would expect that when police performance is consistent with people's expectations, good performance promotes confidence and satisfaction, and verse versa. In the area of police performance, recent studies have highlighted the salient role that procedural justice plays in shaping public trust in the police (Tyler, 2001). It is contended that when people perceive that the police are fair, impartial, recognize citizen rights, and treat people with respect and dignity, they are more likely to trust the police and comply with the law (Sunshine & Tyler, 2003; Tyler, 1990). Further, it is argued that the perceptions of the impartiality of state institutions are of special importance for ethnic minorities, including immigrants, and especially with regard to the treatment of natives versus immigrants (Dinesen, 2012). Fairness is highly underscored because "minorities are evaluating institutional structures that have been created by, are supported by, and affect the majority group" (Kumlin & Rothstein, 2008, p. 12).

There is empirical evidence indicating that the way police handle cases during their encounters mattered more than the occurrence of the encounter itself in determining immigrants' satisfaction (Wu et al., 2011), similar to what was found among the general public (Correia, Reisig, & Lovrich, 1996; Frank, Smith, & Novak, 2005; Skogan, 2005). In one study though, having a police contact itself was associated with less favourable views on the police among a sample of Bangladeshi immigrants (Khondaker et al., 2016). Additionally, although immigrants faced some special problems associated with their status and unfamiliarity with the U.S. justice system, most immigrant victims were satisfied with the treatment accorded them by the police, and when they did have complaints those (such as slow police response times in certain types of crimes like burglary) were the same ones that had been reported in studies of native-born victims (Davis & Henderson, 2003;

Davis, Erez, & Avitabile, 1998). Finally, possibly viewed as an indicator of police incompetence, victimization was found to be associated with lower levels of immigrants' ratings of police effectiveness in one study (Chu et al., 2005), yet not a significant predictor in four other studies (Chu & Song, 2008; Khondaker et al., 2016; Wu et al., 2011; Wu, Smith, & Sun, 2013). As such, it appears direct indicators of the institutional performance theory (i.e., police performance) are more predictive of immigrant confidence in the police than indirect indicators (e.g., victimization, fear of crime).

Universal Variables 3: Structural

Recent research has started to explore how perceptions of the police can vary across areas. Crimes are unevenly distributed amongst locations, and police behaviors also vary by place (Klinger, 1997). Aggregate-level contextual predictors, such as neighborhood racial composition, social class position, extent of physical and social disorder, crime and victimization rates, absence of informal social control, and established patterns of policing, are found to influence residents' levels of satisfaction with the police (e.g., Dai & Johnson, 2009; Reisig & Parks, 2000; Sampson & Bartusch, 1998; Wu et al., 2009). Two theoretical perspectives, the social disorganization theory and the community accountability theory, are helpful in understanding the effects of neighbourhood structural and organizational context and beyond on perceptions of the police.

Social Disorganization Theory

Traditional social disorganization theory posits that neighborhoods with lower levels of poverty, racial heterogeneity, and residential mobility tended to have higher levels of social organization, leading to greater informal social control and lower crime rates (Sampson & Groves, 1989). Based on this theory, residents in neighborhoods with more social, economic, and human resources may hold more positive views toward the police compared to less well-off neighborhoods, perhaps due to lower crime rates, fewer negative contacts between the police and deviant residents, and more opportunities to establish mutual trust between the police and community (Wu et al., 2011). Empirical evidence abounds that concentrated disadvantage, a composite measure that commonly includes indicators of percent minority, percent poor, percent unemployed, and percent female-headed household (Sampson & Bartusch, 1998), was inversely related to satisfaction with the police (Reisig & Parks, 2000). An interaction effect between race and disadvantaged neighborhood context was also noted. Wu et al. (2009) discovered that in socially disadvantaged neighborhoods, Blacks and Whites displayed similar attitudes toward the police, whereas in less disadvantaged neighborhoods Blacks were more likely than Whites to have negative attitudes toward the police. Past studies also showed that neighbourhood crime and disorder conditions influence residents' perceptions of the police with those who live in high crime and/or high incivility neighborhoods more likely to express less favorable views of the police than those living in safer and more ordered communities (Reisig & Parks, 2000; Sampson & Bartusch, 1998). In contrast, the presence of collective efficacy, a concept capturing neighbourhood residents' mutual trust, cohesion, and willingness to intervene, is found to be positively associated with resident perceptions of the police (Wu et al., 2011).

Less than a handful of studies have examined the effects of neighbourhood context on immigrant attitudes toward the police. Regarding collective efficacy, Correia (2010) found no effects of both cohesion and information social control on Latino immigrants' evaluations of the police, while Wu and colleagues found collective efficacy among the most important (positive) predictors of Chinese immigrants' evaluations of the police (Wu et al., 2011, 2013). Meanwhile, immigrants who lived in neighbourhoods with more crime and disorder problems tended to hold less favorable views of the police than their counterparts in safer neighbourhoods (Wu et al., 2011, 2013). In terms of length of residence in a neighbourhood, evidence shows that Latino immigrants who have lived in their current neighbourhood for a longer period of time were more critical of local police than their newer immigrant neighbours (Correia, 2010). It is unclear whether neighborhoods that host more long-term immigrant residents will have on-average more critical views of the police than their counterparts that have more newer immigrant residents.

The Community Accountability Perspective

The community accountability perspective reflects the belief that formal and informal characteristics of police organizations influence police-community relations (Skolnick & Fyfe, 1993). An important effort that aims to improve police accountability to community preferences is to have representative police departments by changing the socio-demographic composition of local police departments to reflect the socio-demographic composition of the larger community being served (Fyfe, 1988; Smith & Holmes, 2003). According to this perspective, greater representation of minorities in the police force will enhance the legitimacy of the police in the eyes of many residents (Smith & Holmes, 2003). A good example may be Dearborn, Michigan, discussed in detail in Chapter 6. The city has highly institutionalized Arab communities, reflected for example by a city council primarily governed by Arab American representatives and a police force led by an Arab American chief. Arab Americans' political prominence and economic prosperity in the area may partially explain their very positive views on their local police (Sun & Wu, 2015). No empirical study has directly tested the effects of racial/ethnic representation or immigrant representation on immigrant perceptions of the police. Although a few jurisdictions (e.g., Chicago and Hawaii) allow immigrants with permanent resident status to join the police force, the vast majority of agencies in the country require police officers to be U.S. citizens (Gomez, 2015, March 21).

Universal Variables 4: Attitudinal

Attitudinal variables reflecting a broad sense of social equity may be the covariates most directly related to people's views of their local police. Particularly, sense of injustice, perceptions of discrimination, and group consciousness are key covariates that merit continued investigation in empirical investigations on immigrant perceptions of the police.

The Sense of Injustice Perspective

The sense of injustice perspective, previously discussed in Chapter 2, proposes that public attitudes toward criminal justice agencies are heavily influenced by their feeling of being treated unjustly by the criminal justice system, including the police along with courts, questions of access to legal representation, and treatment received in the corrections system (Wu et al., 2009). The core arguments of the sense-of-injustice model are in line with the findings from studies on procedural justice which suggest that citizens' perceptions of local legal authorities are heavily influenced by whether they perceive these authorities as fair and equitable in both the procedures for making decisions and the outcomes of the decisions (Tyler, 1990; Tyler & Degoey, 1996). This model emphasizes the state of mind of individuals, with such perceptions, judgment or feelings of the police based on the experience of actual, perceived, or both bias and discrimination in policing. Racial/ethnic minorities tend to display less favorable attitudes toward the police because they are more likely than Whites to perceive unequal treatment by the criminal justice system in general and the police in particular. Institutional procedural fairness therefore is an important force in helping close the trust gap between the majority and the minority as it may have a particularly positive impact among minorities (Hasisi, 2008).

Among minority groups, Black Americans are subject to an extensive and visible history of police oppression and discrimination, and subsequently, are most likely to interpret events through a discrimination frame of reference than other groups (Buckler, Unnever, & Cullen, 2008). Although research findings have not yet provided definitive results concerning the influence of citizen race on police decision making (The National Research Council, 2004), notable racial disparities in various aspects of policing such as police shootings have generated serious concerns about the fairness of law enforcement in America. A massive outcry from African American communities against recent deaths from police violence (Michael Brown, Eric Garner, Tamir Rice, Freddy Gray, Sandra Bland and more) and the advent of the "Black Lives Matter" movement reflect the widespread and deep distrust that Blacks have in the police. Indeed, many African Americans view the police as "occupying armies" in their neighborhoods whose main job is to oppress and control Blacks (Cashmore, 1991).

Compared to Blacks' involuntary immigration in history and the resulting long-standing racial conflict in American society, the majority of Latino and Asian Americans are recent and voluntary immigrants. These new minority groups tend to have a less weighty emotional baggage than that which Blacks carry from long-term conflicts when interacting with the police. Instead, these new minorities often come from home societies where race and ethnicity are much less a "salient, enduring, recognizable, or inflammatory" collective identity than exists in the U.S. (Helms, 1994, p. 187). Owing to the lack of exposure to diversity, they tend to have weaker racial consciousness compared to Blacks, further alleviating their sensitivity to criminal injustice and mitigating their distrust in "White" institutions including the police (Sears & Savalei, 2006). More discussion regarding group consciousness will be provided in a later subsection.

A theory that can be viewed as an important aspect of the sense of injustice thesis is the multifaceted discrimination model, proposed by Van Craen (2013). It argues that people's experiences of discrimination in other aspects of life by other social actors and citizens may erode their overall political trust, including trust in the police (Armstrong et al., 2013; Avery, 2006). Individuals who were victims of discrimination are likely to feel the police, along with other major political institutions, "make too little effort or fail to limit discrimination in society" (Van Craen & Skogan, 2015, p. 8). According to this perspective, immigrants who have encountered injustice including discriminatory treatment, from police officers or others, will hold unfavorable attitudes toward the police. No research on the impact of perceived discrimination on immigrant perceptions of the police can be located to date.

The Group Consciousness Theory

The group consciousness theory suggests that people's trust in political institutions, including the police, is primarily a function of their level of group consciousness. A core dimension of group consciousness is racial consciousness, which "encompasses identification with a racial group and the belief that fundamental differences exist between the power and resources of one's group and those of the dominant group, as well as an understanding that this inequality is illegitimate" (Avery, 2009, p. 133). Racial consciousness is partially a function of racial socialization, a process which features several dimensions of cultural socialization, preparation for experiencing bias, promotion of cautionary mistrust, the principles of egalitarianism, and other belief structures and values (Hughes et al., 2006). The group consciousness theory can be considered as an extension of the group position theory, in that it points out a specific psychological mechanism that connects one's position in society to their political attitudes. By doing so, it also helps to explain the differential attitudes toward the police within the same group of minorities.

According to this theory, minorities who have strong group consciousness are particularly distrustful of the police. Most Blacks, for example, have a strong racial group consciousness, recognizing that race matters in how people are treated and that they will encounter racial discrimination at some point in their lives (Unnever & Gabbidon, 2011). In turn, this consciousness may shape the interactions that Blacks have with the many White-dominated institutions such as schools, colleges and universities, and police, reducing their ability to trust in and bond with these institutions (Tate, 2010; Unnever & Gabbidon, 2011).

Some groups, such as foreign-born Mexican and Asian Americans, tend to have weaker group consciousness, coming from more homogeneous societies and entering the country with only limited knowledge on racial relations and historical struggles, which may contribute to their more positive views of the police when compared to African Americans (Portes & Rumbaut, 2001; Wu, 2014). In fact, even within the African American population differential levels of institutional trust exist depending on one's level of race consciousness. Avery (2006) found, of example, that mistrust in government is strongest among Blacks who have strong racial identification and believe racial disparities and discrimination is still a problem in various arenas of American life. In addition, Black immigrants have notable differences in levels of racial consciousness from African Americans. For Afro-Caribbean immigrants, race was not a salient dimension of identity in the Caribbean region (Vickerman, 2001). Many have had a hard time getting used to race being a "central axis of social relation" in the U.S. (Omi & Winant, 1986, p. 61). Regardless of experiences with racial discrimination, immigrant Blacks are much "less likely than native-born blacks to argue that racism and structural obstacles negatively affect the position of blacks in the United States" (Benson, 2006, p. 225). Thus, while there is a nearly universal perception among native-born Black Americans that the criminal justice system is "racist" to a large degree, this core belief is not fully shared by foreign-born Blacks, persons of color who are significantly less likely to believe that the criminal justice system treats Blacks and Whites unequally (Unnever & Gabbidon, 2015).

Immigrant-Specific Variables 1: Demographic

For immigrant minorities, in addition to race and ethnicity there are two other noteworthy individual characteristics, *immigrant status* (foreign-born v. US-born) and the *degree of assimilation*, which should be considered to be key facets of identity.

The Immigrant Paradox Thesis

The immigrant paradox thesis has been proposed to describe "the counterintuitive finding that immigrants have better adaptation outcomes than their national peers despite their poorer socioeconomic conditions" (Sam, Vedder, Ward, & Horenczyk, 2006, p. 125). That is, although on average more economically, politically and socially disadvantaged, many immigrant groups outperform their native-born counterparts, including similarly disadvantaged African Americans, in various areas of academic achievement, personal health, and psychological wellbeing. Likewise, they tend to engage in lower rates of violence, smoking and drug use, and display fewer other problem behaviors (Desmond & Kubrin, 2009; Fuligni, 1998; MacDonald & Saunders, 2012; Sam et al., 2006; Wright & Benson, 2010). Immigrant Blacks, for example, are deemed by some as America's "new model minority" group (Freeman, 2002). They, especially African-born Blacks, reported higher levels of physical and emotional wellbeing and educational achievement than native-born Blacks, and sometimes native Latinos and Whites as well (Crosnoe & Turley-Lopez, 2011; Logan, 2007; Thomas, 2012; Wheeler, Brooks, & Brown, 2011). There is also evidence indicating that foreign-born Blacks (e.g., Haitians) have lower rates of arrest than U.S.-born Blacks (Nielsen & Martinez, 2011).

Criminologists have suggested that protective factors, such as neighborhood informal social control, social networks, cultural norms, and expectations about migration and life overall, may contribute to the lower rates of crime and violence among immigrant groups despite their vulnerability in the foreign country (Desmond & Kubrin, 2009; Wright & Benson, 2010). There is also an argument made by some scholars that the relative success of first-generation immigrants is to some extent a result of government selective screening practices on who can enter and stay in this nation legally. Relatedly, there is most certainly some effect of individuals' self-selection, with those who are most healthy and most highly motivated migrating to the U.S. and less able and motivated persons remaining put (Jasso, Massey, Rosenzweig, & Smith, 2004). Finally, preliminary evidence has been reported suggesting that immigrants, compared to their native-born counterparts, are subject to somewhat lower risks of crime victimization (Wu & Altheimer, 2013). All these elements might create a cultural synchronicity that leads immigrants to be more confident in police protection, and more trustful of police officers and the institution of the police in the U.S., compared to their country of origin.

Empirical evidence on the immigrant paradox thesis have been mixed. Davis and Hendricks (2007), relying on a Seattle sample, revealed that immigrants (primarily Latino and Asian) had more favorable assessments of the police than non-immigrants in several such areas as integrity, fairness, and effectiveness. Another study conducted with Latino immigrants in Reno, Nevada, also showed that immigrants had more favourable views of the police than non-immigrants in various evaluative areas of fairness, honesty, and equal treatments (Correia, 2010). In contrast, Wu and colleagues (2011) found that foreign-born Chinese immigrants displayed a significantly lower level of satisfaction with police effectiveness and demeanour than their U.S.-born counterparts, failing to support the immigrant paradox thesis.

Finally, a study in Chicago found that Spanish-speaking Latinos held similar views of the police as English-speaking Latinos in about half of their thirteen evaluative questions and rated police slightly more negatively than English-speaking Latinos in the remaining seven questions (Skogan, Steiner, DuBois, Gudeel, & Fagan, 2002). The researchers concluded that foreign-born residents' views of the Chicago police did not differ much from native-born Chicagoans.

The Theory of Assimilation

The classical theory of assimilation portrayed the assimilation process as an integral part of the successful movement of immigrant groups into the American middle class (Warner & Srole, 1945). As immigrants become more acculturated into the host society, the theory predicted that they would experience improved socioeconomic status, leading them to develop more positive views toward their host society's institutions—including the police. Many scholars, however, have argued that the classical theory of assimilation is no longer applicable to the new immigrant groups, including those who are primarily from Asia and Latin America since 1960s, because it appears that children of new immigrant groups often perform less well compared to their parents' generations (Gans, 1992). For example, early engagement in risky behaviors, including delinquency and substance abuse, are more common among second-generation immigrants than among their first generation counterparts (Harris, 1999; Nagasawa, Qian, & Wong, 2001; Rumbaut, 1997; Zhou & Bankston, 1998). One of the main alternatives to the classical theory of assimilation, "segmented assimilation," holds that immigrant children may actually benefit from delayed or strategically selective assimilation (Portes & Rumbaut, 2001; Portes & Zhou, 1993).

Empirical research on the effects of degree of assimilation on immigrant perceptions of the police has mainly examined the effects of English proficiency and length of residence. Some researchers have found that English proficiency was positively related to perceptions of police helpfulness, concern, fairness, and responsiveness to neighborhood problems (Skogan et al., 2002). Other researchers have reported an opposite pattern, noting that in some settings immigrants who had better English communication skills reported lower evaluations of the police (Correia, 2010), and likewise reported less comfort in cooperating with the police (Cheurprakobkit & Bartsch, 1999). Still others found language proficiency to *not* be predictive of immigrants' satisfaction with the police (Khondaker et al., 2016), of perceptions of police bias or prejudice (Wu et al., 2013; Chu & Song, 2015), of respect for the police, or of assessments of police effectiveness and rapid response (Chu & Song, 2015).

The effects of length of residence in the U.S. are likewise mixed. Some researchers found no significant effect on immigrants' satisfaction with the police, perceptions of police prejudice, effectiveness, integrity, or provision of adequate protection (Chu & Song, 2015; Khondaker et al., 2016; Wu et al., 2011). However, other researchers discovered the presence of some curvilinear effects on perceptions of police bias (Wu et al., 2013), with newcomers who have been in this country for less than three years having the most positive views, followed by long-term residents, while immigrants who have resided in the U.S. for a median period of time (4–14 years) had the least positive views on police equal treatment. It is speculated that these attitudinal variations may reflect the varied stages of the assimilation process experienced by the Chinese immigrants studied. Among Chinese immigrants the original optimism holds up for short-termers, the growing racial consciousness that follows for medium-termers is associated with some waning of this optimism, and eventually the Americanized process associated with improved alienated group status serves as a good description for long-termers (Wu et al., 2013). This pattern may (or may not) apply to other immigrant groups, as there is evidence indicating that foreign-born Latinos feel more politically alienated over time in the U.S., with such feelings being correlated with perceptions of discrimination (Michelson, 2003).

Immigrant-Specific Variables 2: Experiential

Immigrants often have unique traumatic life experiences that their native-born counterparts do not have. Three such experiential variables may be relevant in studying their attitudes toward the U.S. police: experience with home country police, perceptions of home country crime conditions, and experience with U.S. immigration officers.

The Imported Socialization Theory

The imported socialization theory holds that immigrants bring along with them to the host country their primary socialization occurring in their home society prior to their resettlement. Such imported socialization likely affects their political behavior (Wals, 2011), and quite possibly affects their expectations and evaluations of the host society institutions as well. As Suarez-Orozco (1990) has argued persuasively, immigrants typically bring with them their understanding of the social institutions and processes which affected them in their home country, using that as references to interpret their experiences in the new country to which they migrate.

Preliminary findings from the few studies available suggest that immigrants' perceptions of their home country police do exert some influence on their attitudes toward police effectiveness and integrity in their host country. Positive evaluations of home country police, for example, were associated with higher ratings of the U.S. police among Chinese and Korean immigrants in the U.S. (Pogrebin & Poole, 1990; Wu et al., 2011). Trust in the Mexican government was also found to correspond with trust in the U.S. government among Mexican immigrants (Wals, 2011). These results seem to suggest two possibilities, either that individuals have a relatively stable "propensity" in their evaluations of and sentiments toward the police, or individuals may "transfer" their evaluations and sentiments from one country to another. One study, however, reported an opposite pattern, noting that negative perceptions of home country police were associated with greater faith in the U.S. police among crime victims from multiple immigrant groups in both New York and Philadelphia (Davis et al., 1998). Finally, a study on Bangladeshi immigrants in New York revealed no significant effects of either personal or vicarious contact with home police on their evaluations of the host country police (Khondasker et al., 2016).

The Contrast Thesis

Advocates of contrast thesis argue that favorable contrast creates affection. Just as warmth is best appreciated in the dead of winter, and peace is most cherished in times of war, highly professional and democratic policing is most greatly appreciated by those immigrants coming from authoritarian societies where the police often abuse their power. People's sentiments toward crime and justice too are likely based on their pre-existing experiences, attitudes, and store of information (Ferraro, 1995). For immigrants, a substantial portion of their pre-existing experiences and attitudes pertain to pre-migration, and it is possible that a positive contrast between home and host society crime situation (i.e., crime conditions are better in the host society compared to the home society) can lead to more positive views of police performance in the host country.

There is some indirect empirical support for this argument. Furr and associates (2005) discovered that refugees from the former Soviet Union had significantly higher levels of perceived safety than the general public in Louisville, Kentucky. The old risks of living in a negative environment of social chaos and economic decline outweighed the new risks of living in a foreign country with unfamiliar norms and fewer familiar social networks. Another study, based on a sample of Chinese immigrants settled in metro-Detroit, found that perception of crime seriousness in one's home city was negatively associated with fear of crime in the host city (Wu & Wen, 2014). Of course, applying the contrast thesis to explaining the differential attitudes toward the police found in these two studies is based on a premise that people's fear of crime has a significant relationship to their perceptions of the police, which received only inconsistent support from the general public's perceptions of the police literature (see Brown & Benedict, 2002).

The Trust-Transference Hypothesis

The trust-transference hypothesis posits that people's trust in law enforcement personnel besides the police may well affect their trust in the police. When immigrants first interact with an employee in the law enforcement sector, such as a border patrol officer or an immigration official, they form their first perceptions of whether the law enforcement system can be trusted. Once the trust (or mistrust) in the law enforcement system is established, that same trust may be translated into trust in another employee of the system, such as the local police. Importantly, immigrants' attitudes toward the police may be particularly affected by their experience with U.S. immigration officers. Not all immigrants have direct experience with the police, yet almost all have some substantive experience with U.S. immigration officials (Wu et al., 2011). Some immigrants, particularly those from countries with centralized civil service systems and those at a young age, may not distinguish between police officers and immigration officers. Adding to this confusion, in the post-9/11 era many local police departments have become involved in the enforcement of federal immigration laws (Skogan, 2009). The blurring of roles between immigration officials and local police may add to immigrants' fear of and mistrust of the police in general. Preliminary evidence shows that there is indeed a significantly positive link between immigrants' assessments of the U.S. immigration officials and the services they provide and their attitudes toward local police in multiple evaluative areas (Wu et al., 2011). Relatedly, immigrants' fear of deportation resulting from contacts with the police is found to be associated with lower satisfaction with the local police (Khondasker et al., 2016; Skogan, 2009; Vidales, Day, & Powe, 2009).

Immigrant-Specific Variables 3: Structural

Perceived from a somewhat broader perspective, matters of the police-community relationship can also be related to the fabric of social structure of any given society. As previously noted, neighborhood and city contextual factors can contribute to the formation of individual views on the police. For immigrants, their trust and satisfaction with the U.S. police may be influenced by the very society or culture from which they originate. Perhaps the foremost structural variable research on immigrant perceptions of the police needs to take into account is the nature of the regime from which immigrants come.

The Critical Citizen Thesis

The critical citizen thesis posits that during the past few decades many democratic countries have experienced an increase in the number of critical citizens who are less trustful and deferential to authorities, and more ready to challenge them (Norris, 1999; Pharr & Putnam, 2000). Accordingly, immigrants from these Western democratic countries may hold more critical views on government agencies, including the police, than their counterparts from less democratic regimes. Indeed, Gibson and Duch (1994) found in their study of European Community countries that immigrants from countries lacking long-established democratic traditions are more likely to exhibit trust in the political system. It is argued that in an authoritarian regime, perhaps because of the more pervasive and forceful role of the state, individuals develop greater trust, as well as more authoritarian values, consonant with their favorable attitudes toward authoritarian figures such as the police. Alternatively, according to the arguments of the contrast thesis, the higher levels of political trust among immigrants from authoritarian regimes may also result from a contrast between the old and the new regimes, leading immigrants to come to appreciate and support democratic policing in their host country.

It is worth noting that police experience of a non-democratic country early in life may have a more substantial impact on values than that of similar democratic experiences, especially when such experience of early socialization was a lengthy one (McAllister & Makkai, 1992). Finally, immigrants from some Western democratic countries may be more trustful of the police than others. Specifically, those from the modern welfare states, such as the Scandinavian countries, may have higher levels of trust than those from developed countries with greater social inequalities, such as Israel. This may be the case because the equality and social welfare prevalent in those social-democratic or universal welfare state regimes can better meet people's perceptions and expectations of procedural fairness, expectations which are especially conductive to strengthening people's political trust (Kumlin, 2004; Zmerli, 2012).

Immigrant-Specific Variables 4: Attitudinal

Closely related to the structural dimension is the cultural dimension of influencers of public attitudes toward the police. Culture develops around structure, yet may serve as the more direct or immediate influencer upon public perceptions of the police, compared to structure.

The Cultural Thesis

A few specific cultural traits may be particularly relevant to the matters of police-citizen interactions, and the development of the relationship obtaining between the police and the citizens they serve. For example, *power distance*, a sociological concept pertaining to the cultural relationship between superiors and subordinates (Hofstede, 2001), may affect public attitudes toward the police; in a high power distance society citizens may fear and respect the police more than in a low power distance Western society. Similarly, according to Schwartz's (2006) theory of cultural value orientations, some cultures, such as the Chinese, are very high in the dimensions of hierarchical distribution of roles and individual compliance with these roles, but very low in egalitarianism which emphasizes moral equals, social justice, and responsibility among people. Accordingly, people from such countries as China may attach greater importance to obeying the rules and carrying out orders from the police than insisting upon the observance of individual rights and the provision of equal protection to all persons. Consequently, those persons having a Chinese heritage may have quite different expectations of police performance than immigrants from a less hierarchical and more equalitarian cultural background. In sum, this perspective argues that as different immigrant groups come with varied cultural traits and historical legacies, they may hold widely differing political and social attitudes, including perceptions of the proper conduct of the police. Empirical research on the effects of cultural traits on immigrant perceptions of the police is lacking. Conceptualization and operationalization of such cultural predictors remain a challenge.

Future Testing of the Conceptual Model

As with all social science theories, those discussed in this chapter are better understood as models that work in a limited range of settings rather than laws of science that hold and apply universally across geographic space and time (Turner, 2009). Needless to say, among those discussed in this chapter, some are more general than others and enjoy greater empirical support. According to the positivistic conception of science, a good theory is one that has *parsimony* (the ability to explain in relatively few terms and statements), *generalizability* (the ability to explain a breadth of phenomena), *accuracy* (the ability to accurately predict new phenomena), and *falsifiability* (the ability to be disproved). Future research should empirically test these theories and critically evaluate their parsimony, generalizability, accuracy, and falsifiability. These theories, in addition, may be very useful for future researchers to develop their own conceptual frameworks and analytical models.

For future research, it will be a potentially fruitful endeavor to evaluate the relative strength of different explanations. As some theories complement one another, it will also be worthwhile for scholars to develop and test integrated models based on two or more of these theories that share common assumptions. In addition, different theories may explain different immigrant groups better or less well, depending on group culture and other broadly shared collective experiences. Indeed, as each individual holds a position in different systems of social stratification simultaneously, an *intersectional* framework of studying group perceptions of the police based on race, ethnicity, and culture, while at the same time incorporating other important factors that this conceptual model proposes, will have great value. Moreover, it is quite important to take a developmental perspective on public, particularly immigrant minority, perceptions of the police in the U.S. Factors that come to influence people's perceptions may change over time; for example, different theories may be particularly relevant to distinctive stages of the life course. Finally, valid and reliable measures need to be developed and tested to capture those very subtle and complicated historical, social and cultural elements of public perception. The convergence of "hard" methodological approaches with "soft" behavioral variables will continue to be a challenging yet far-reaching goal.

These proposed ideas for future research are demanding ones, but sorely needed to build a truly democratic policing legacy in a country of rapidly growing cultural, racial and ethnic diversity. At the very least, it is hoped that this conceptual model can spark more interest in theoretically-guided empirical research on immigrant minority perceptions of the police.

Summary

This chapter systematically reviews the existing research literature that compares attitudes toward the police across minority groups, and innovatively proposes a theoretical framework that can help explain immigrant group differences in attitudes toward the U.S. police. The currently dominant binary Black/White paradigm in research on crime and criminal justice in the U.S. has serious limitations in the face of the greatly enhanced demographic diversity of the country. Waves of immigration, particularly those from Latin America and Asia, have added new dimensions to the complexity of race and ethnicity issues in the country. Any serious effort to provide a foundation for a comprehensive account of American police-community relations thus requires attention to the experience of immigrant minorities.

This chapter delineates a number of existing and new theoretical perspectives that may be useful for explaining group differential views on the police between immigrants and non-immigrants and among immigrant groups. Particularly, we formulate a conceptual framework for classifying these theories. Theories are first organized by the two sources of influence that immigrant attitudes toward the police are subject to: universal factors that shape all residents' attitudes toward the police, and group-specific factors that only apply to foreign-born individuals. Then within both universal and immigrant-specific factors, there are four subcategories of demographic, experiential, structural, and attitudinal variables. Future research should build upon components of this model and carry out serious efforts of theory falsification, competition, and integration. Developing and improving theoretical understanding of both shared and divergent paths in police-community relations across different racial, ethnic, and immigrant groups should be a primary goal for scholars interested in race, immigration, and policing.

References

Armstrong, K., Putt, M., Halbert, C., Grande, D., Schwartz, J., Liao, K., Shea, J. (2013). Prior experiences of racial discrimination and racial differences in health care system distrust. *Medical Care, 51,* 144–150.

Avery, J. (2006). The sources and consequences of political mistrust among African Americans. *American Politics Research, 34,* 653–682.

Avery, J. (2009). Political mistrust among African Americans and support for the political system. *Political Research Quarterly, 62,* 132–145.

Bender, L., & Braveman, D. (1995). *Power, privilege, and law: A civil rights reader.* St. Paul, MN: West Publishing Company.

Benson, J. (2006). Exploring the racial identities of Black immigrants in the United States. *Sociological Forum, 21,* 219–247.

Berg, J. (2010). Race, class, gender, and social space: Using an intersectional approach to study immigration attitudes. *The Sociological Quarterly, 51,* 278–302.

Blalock, H. (1967). *Toward a theory of minority-group relations.* New York: Wiley.

Blumer, H. (1958). Race prejudice as a sense of group position. *Pacific Sociological Review, 1,* 3–7.

Bobo, L. (1999). Prejudice as group position. *Journal of Social Issues, 55,* 445–472.

Bobo, L., & Hutchings, V. (1996). Perceptions of racial group competition: Extending Blumer's theory of group position to a multiracial social context. *American Sociological Review, 61,* 951–972.

Bobo, L., & Tuan, M. (2006). *Prejudice in politics: Group position, public opinion, and the Wisconsin treaty rights dispute.* Cambridge, MA: Harvard University Press.

Brown, B., & Benedict, W. (2002). Perceptions of the police: Past findings, methodological issues, conceptual issues and policy implications. *Policing: An International Journal of Police Strategies & Management, 25,* 543–580.

Browning, S., & Cao, L. (1992). The impact of race on criminal justice ideology. *Justice Quarterly, 9,* 685–702.

Buckler, K., & Unnever, J. (2008). Racial and ethnic perceptions of injustice: Testing the core hypotheses of comparative conflict theory. *Journal of Crime and Justice, 36,* 270–278.

Buckler, K., Unnever, J., & Cullen, F. (2008). Perceptions of injustice revisited: A test of Hagan et al.'s comparative conflict theory. *Journal of Criminal Justice, 31,* 35–57.

Cashmore, E. (1991). Black cops, Inc. In E. Cashmore & E. McLaughlin (Eds.), *Out of order: Policing black people* (pp. 97–108). New York: Routledge.

Cheurprakobkit, S., & Bartsch, R. (1999). Police work and the police profession: Assessing attitudes of city officials, Spanish-speaking Hispanics, and their English-speaking counterparts. *Journal of Criminal Justice, 27,* 87–100.

Chu, D., & Song, J. (2008). Chinese immigrants' perceptions of the police in Toronto, Canada. *Policing: An International Journal of Police Strategies and Management, 31,* 610–630.

Chu, D., & Song, J. (2015). A comparison of Chinese immigrants' perceptions of the police in New York City and Toronto. *Crime & Delinquency, 61,* 402–427.

Chu, D., Song, J., & Dombrink, J. (2005). Chinese immigrants' perceptions of the police in New York City. *International Criminal Justice Review, 15,* 101–114.

Correia, M. (2010). Determinants of attitudes toward police of Latino immigrants and non-immigrants. *Journal of Criminal Justice, 38,* 99–107.

Correia, M., Reisig, M., & Lovrich, N. (1996). Public perceptions of state police: An analysis of individual-level and contextual variables. *Journal of Criminal Justice, 24,* 17–28.

Crosnoe, R., & Turley-Lopez, R. (2011). K-12 educational outcomes of immigrant youth. *The Future of Children, 21,* 129–152.

Dai, M., & Johnson, R. (2009). Is neighborhood context a confounder? Exploring the effects of citizen race and neighborhood context on satisfaction with the police. *Policing: An International Journal of Police Strategies & Management, 32,* 595–612.

Davis, R., Erez, E., & Avitabile, N. (1998). Immigrants and the criminal justice system: An exploratory study. *Violence and Victims, 13,* 21–30.

Davis, R., & Henderson, N. (2003). Willingness to report crimes: The role of ethnic group membership and community efficacy. *NCCD News, 49,* 564–580.

Davis, R., & Hendricks, N. (2007). Immigrants and law enforcement: A comparison of native-born and foreign-born Americans' opinions of the police. *International Review of Victimology, 14,* 81–94.

Desmond, S., & Kubrin, C. (2009). The power of place: Immigrant communities and adolescent violence. *The Sociological Quarterly, 50,* 581–607.

Dinesen, P. (2012). Parental transmission of trust or perceptions of institutional fairness: Generalized trust of non-Western immigrants in a high-trust society. *Comparative Politics, 44,* 273–289.

Feagin, J. (2013). *The white racial frame: Centuries of racial framing and counter-framing* (2nd ed.). New York: Routledge.

Feinstein, R. (2015). A qualitative analysis of police interactions and disproportionate minority contact. *Journal of Ethnicity in Criminal Justice, 13,* 159–178.

Ferraro, K. (1995). *Fear of crime: Interpreting victimization risk.* Albany, NY: SUNY Press.

Frank, J., Smith, B., & Novak, K. (2005). Exploring the basis of citizens' attitudes toward the police. *Police Quarterly, 8,* 206–228.

Freeman, L. (2002). Does spatial assimilation work for black immigrants in the US? *Urban Studies, 39,* 1983–2003.

Fuligni, A. (1998). The adjustment of children from immigrant families. *Current Directions in Psychological Science, 7,* 99–103.

Furr, A., Austin, M., Cribbs, S., & Smoger, S. (2005). The effects of neighborhood satisfaction on perception of safety among refugees from the former Soviet Union. *Sociological Spectrum, 25,* 519–537.

Fyfe, J. (1988). Police use of deadly force: Research and reform. *Justice Quarterly, 5,* 165–205.

Gabbidon, S., & Greene, H. (Eds.). (2013). *Race, crime, and justice: A reader.* New York: Routledge.

Gans, H. (1992). Second-generation decline: Scenarios for the economic and ethnic futures of the post-1965 American immigrants. *Ethnic and Racial Studies, 15,* 173–192.

Garcia, V., & Cao, L. (2005). Race and satisfaction with the police in a small city. *Journal of Criminal Justice, 33,* 191–199.

Gibson, J., & Duch, R. (1994). Support for rights in Western Europe and the Soviet Union: An analysis of the beliefs of mass publics. In F. Weil (Ed.), *Research on democracy and society: Democratization in Eastern and Western Europe*. Greenwich, CT: JAI Press.

Gomez, A. (2015, March 21). Police departments hiring immigrants as officers. *USA Today*, Accessed December 25, 2017 at https://www.usatoday.com/story/news/nation/2015/03/21/immigrant-police-officers/70236828/.

Harris, K. (1999). The health status and risk behaviors of adolescents in immigrant families. In D. Hernandez (Eds.), *Children of immigrants: Health, adjustment, and public assistance* (pp. 286–347). Washington, DC: National Academy Press.

Hasisi, B. (2008). Police politics, and culture. *Journal of Criminal Law and Criminology, 98*, 1119–1146.

Helms, J. (1994). The conceptualization of racial identity and other "racial" constructs. In E. Trickett, R. Watts, & D. Birman (Eds.), *Human diversity: Perspectives on people in context* (pp. 285–311). San Francisco, CA: Jossey-Bass.

Hofstede, G. (2001). *Culture's consequences: Comparing values, behaviours, institutions, and organizations across nations*. Thousand Oaks, CA: Sage.

Holmes, M., & Smith, B. (2008). *Race and police brutality: Roots of an urban dilemma*. Albany, NY: State University of New York Press.

Hughes, D., Rodriguez, J., Smith, E. P., Johnson, D. J., Stevenson, H. C., & Spicer, P. (2006). Parents' ethnic–Racial socialization practices: A review of research and directions for future study. *Developmental Psychology, 42*, 747–770.

Jasso, G., Massey, D., Rosenzweig, M., & Smith, J. (2004). Immigrant health: Selectivity and acculturation. In N. Anderson, R. Bulatao, & B. Cohen (Eds.), *Critical perspectives on racial and ethnic differences in health in late life* (pp. 227–266). Washington, DC: The National Academies Press, National Research Council.

Khondaker, M., Wu, Y., & Lambert, E. (2016). The views of Bangladeshi immigrants on the U.S. police. *Journal of Crime and Justice, 39*, 528–549.

Kim, C. (2004). Imagining race and nation in multiculturalist America. *Ethnic and Racial Studies, 27*, 987–1005.

Klinger, D. (1997). Negotiating order in patrol work: An ecological theory of police response to deviance. *Criminology, 35*, 277–306.

Kumlin, S. (2004). *The personal and the political: How personal welfare state experiences affect political trust and ideology*. New York: Palgrave.

Kumlin, S., & Rothstein, B. (2008). *Minorities and mistrust: The cushioning impact of social contacts and institutional fairness* (The quality of government institute working paper series 18). Accessed February 12, 2016 at http://qog.pol.gu.se/digitalAssets/1350/1350670_2008_18_kumlin_rothstein.pdf.

Lai, Y., & Zhao, J. (2010). The impact of race/ethnicity, neighborhood context, and police/citizen interaction on residents' attitudes toward the police. *Journal of Criminal Justice, 38*, 685–692.

Logan, J. (2007). Who are the other African Americans? Contemporary African and Caribbean immigrants in the United States. In Y. Shaw-Taylor & S. Tuch (Eds.), *The other African Americans: Contemporary African and Caribbean immigrants in the United States* (pp. 49–68). Lanham, MD: Rowman & Littlefield.

MacDonald, J., & Saunders, J. (2012). Are immigrant youth less violent? Specifying the reasons and mechanisms. *The Annals of the American Academy of Political and Social Science, 641*, 125–147.

McAllister, I., & Makkai, T. (1992). Resource and social learning theories of political participation: Ethnic patterns in Australia. *Canadian Journal of Political Science, 25*, 269–293.

Michelson, M. (2003). The corrosive effect of acculturation: How Mexican Americans lose political trust. *Social Science Quarterly, 84*, 918–933.

Nagasawa, R., Qian, Z., & Wong, P. (2001). Theory of segmented assimilation and the adoption of marijuana use and delinquent behavior by Asian Pacific youth. *The Sociological Quarterly, 42*, 351–372.

National Research Council (NRC). (2004). In W. Skogan & K. Frydl (Eds.), *Fairness and effectiveness in policing: The evidence*. Washington, DC: The National Academies Press.

Nielsen, A., & Martinez, R. (2011). Nationality, immigrant groups, and arrest: Examining the diversity of arrestees for urban violent crime. *Journal of Contemporary Criminal Justice, 27*, 342–360.

Norris, P. (1999). *Critical citizens: Global support for democratic government*. Oxford: Oxford University Press.

Omi, M., & Winant, H. (1986). *Racial formation in the United States*. New York: Routledge.

Pager, D., & Shepherd, H. (2008). The sociology of discrimination: Racial discrimination in employment, housing, credit, and consumer markets. *Annual Review of Sociology, 34*, 181–209.

Peck, J. (2015). Minority perceptions of the police: A state-of-the-art review. *Policing: An International Journal of Police Strategies & Management, 38*, 173–203.

Pharr, S., & Putnam, R. (2000). *Disaffected democracies: What's troubling the trilateral countries?* Princeton, NJ: Princeton University Press.

Pogrebin, M., & Poole, E. (1990). Cultural conflict and crime in the Korean American community. *Criminal Justice Policy Review, 4*, 69–78.

Portes, A., & Rumbaut, R. (2001). *Legacies: The story of the immigrant second generation.* Berkeley, CA: University of California Press.

Portes, A., & Zhou, M. (1993). The new second generation: Segmented assimilation and its variants. *The Annals of the American Academy of Political and Social Sciences, 530*, 74–96.

Reisig, M., & Parks, R. (2000). Experience, quality of life, and neighborhood context: A hierarchical analysis of satisfaction with police. *Justice Quarterly, 17*, 607–630.

Rumbaut, R. (1997). Assimilation and its discontents: Between rhetoric and reality. *The International Migration Review, 31*, 923–960.

Sam, D., Vedder, P., Ward, C., & Horenczyk, G. (2006). Psychological and sociocultural adaptation of immigrant youth. In J. Berry, J. Phinney, D. Sam, & P. Vedder (Eds.), *Immigrant youth in cultural transition: Acculturation, identity, and adaptation across national contexts* (pp. 132–142). Mahwah, NJ: Lawrence Erlbaum Associates.

Sampson, R., & Bartusch, D. (1998). Legal cynicism and (subcultural?) tolerance of deviance: The neighborhood context of racial differences. *Law and Society Review, 32*, 777–804.

Sampson, R., & Groves, W. (1989). Community structure and crime: Testing social-disorganization theory. *American Journal of Sociology, 94*, 774–802.

Schafer, J., Huebner, B., & Bynum, T. (2003). Citizen perceptions of police services: Race, neighborhood context, and community policing. *Police Quarterly, 6*, 440–468.

Schuck, A., & Rosenbaum, D. (2005). Global and neighborhood attitudes toward the police: Differentiation by race, ethnicity and type of contact. *Journal of Quantitative Criminology, 21*, 391–418.

Schwartz, S. (2006). A theory of cultural value orientations: Explication and applications. *Comparative Sociology, 5*, 137–182.

Sears, D., & Savalei, V. (2006). The political color line in America: many "peoples of color" or black exceptionalism? *Political Psychology, 27*, 895–924.

Skogan, W. (2005). Citizen satisfaction with police encounters. *Police Quarterly, 8*, 298–321.

Skogan, W. (2009). Policing immigrant communities in the United States. *Sociology of Crime, Law and Deviance, 13*, 189–203.

Skogan, W., Steiner, L., DuBois, J., Gudeel, E., & Fagan, A. (2002). *Community policing and "the new immigrants": Latinos in Chicago.* Evanston, IL: Institute for Police Research, Northwestern University.

Skolnick, J., & Fyfe, J. (1993). *Above the law: Police and the excessive use of force* (pp. 43–48). New York: Free Press.

Smith, B., & Holmes, M. (2003). Community accountability, minority threat, and police brutality: An examination of civil rights criminal complaints. *Criminology, 41,* 1035–1063.

Song, J. (1992). Attitudes of Chinese immigrants and Vietnamese refugees toward law enforcement in the United States. *Justice Quarterly, 9,* 703–719.

Suarez-Orozco, M. (1990). Migration and education: United States–Europe comparison. In G. De Vos & M. Suarez-Orozco (Eds.), *Status inequality: The self in culture* (pp. 265–287). Thousand Oaks, CA: Sage.

Sun, I., & Wu, Y. (2015). Arab Americans' confidence in police. *Crime & Delinquency, 61,* 483–508.

Sunshine, J., & Tyler, T. (2003). The role of procedural justice and legitimacy in shaping public support for policing. *Law and Society Review, 37,* 513–548.

Tate, K. (2010). *What's going on: Political incorporation and the transformation of Black public opinion.* Washington, DC: Georgetown University Press.

Taylor, T., Turner, K., Esbensen, F., & Winfree, L., Jr. (2001). Coppin' an attitude: Attitudinal differences among juveniles toward police. *Journal of Criminal Justice, 29,* 501–521.

Thomas, J. (2012). Race and school enrollment among the children of African immigrants in the United States. *International Migration Review, 46,* 37–60.

Torres, S., & Vogel, R. (2001). Pre- and post-test differences between Vietnamese and Latino residents involved in a community policing experiment: Reducing fear of crime and improving attitudes toward the police. *Policing: An International Journal of Police Strategies and Management, 24,* 40–55.

Turner, S. (2009). Theory development and construction. In J. McKinlay & L. Marceau (Eds.), *Behavioral and social science research interactive textbook.* Washington, DC: Office of Behavioral and Social Science Research, National Institutes of Health.

Twomey, B. (2001). Labour market participation of ethnic groups. *Labour Market Trends, 109,* 29–42.

Tyler, T. (1990). *Why people obey the law.* New Haven, CT: Yale University Press.

Tyler, T. (2001). Public trust and confidence in legal authorities: What do majority and minority group members want from the law and legal authorities? *Behavioral Sciences & the Law, 19,* 215–235.

Tyler, T., & Degoey, P. (1996). Trust in organizational authorities. The influence of motive attributions on willingness to accept decisions. In R. Kramer & T. Tyler (Eds.), *Trust in organizations: Frontiers of theory and research* (pp. 331–355). Thousand Oaks, CA: Sage.

Unnever, J., & Gabbidon, S. (2011). *A theory of African American offending: Race, racism, and crime.* New York: Routledge.

Unnever, J., & Gabbidon, S. (2015). Do Blacks speak with one voice? Immigrants, public opinions, and perceptions of criminal injustices. *Justice Quarterly, 32,* 680–704.

Van Craen, M. (2013). Explaining majority and minority trust in the police. *Justice Quarterly, 30,* 1042–1067.

Van Craen, M., & Skogan, W. (2015). Differences and similarities in the explanation of ethnic minority groups' trust in the police. *European Journal of Criminology, 12,* 300–323.

Vickerman, M. (2001). Jamaicans: Balancing race and ethnicity. In N. Foner (Ed.), *New immigrants in New York* (pp. 201–228). New York: Columbia University Press.

Vidales, G., Day, K., & Powe, M. (2009). Police and immigration enforcement: Impact on Latino(a) residents' perceptions of police. *Policing: An International Journal of Police Strategies & Management, 32,* 631–653.

Walker, S. (1997). Complaints against the police: A focus group study of citizen perceptions, goals and expectations. *Criminal Justice Review, 22,* 207–226.

Wals, S. (2011). Does what happen in Los Mochis stay in Los Mochis? Explaining post migration political behavior. *Political Research Quarterly, 64,* 600–611.

Warner, W., & Srole, L. (1945). *The social systems of American ethnic groups.* New Haven, CT: Yale University Press.

Webb, V., & Marshall, C. (1995). The relative importance of race and ethnicity on citizen attitudes toward the police. *American Journal of Police, 14,* 45–66.

Weitzer, R. (2002). Incidents of police misconduct and public opinion. *Journal of Criminal Justice, 30,* 397–408.

Weitzer, R., & Tuch, S. (2006). *Race and policing in America: Conflict and reform.* New York: Cambridge University Press.

Wheeler, E., Brooks, L., & Brown, J. (2011). "Gettin' on my last nerve": Mental health, physiological and cognitive implications of racism for people of African descent. *The Journal of Pan African Studies, 4,* 81–101.

Wilson, J. (1975). *Thinking about crime.* New York: Vintage.

Wilson, W. (1978). *The declining significance of race.* Chicago, IL: University of Chicago Press.

Wright, E., & Benson, M. (2010). Immigration and intimate partner violence: Exploring the immigrant paradox. *Social Problems, 57,* 480–503.

Wu, Y. (2014). Race/ethnicity and perceptions of the police: A comparison of White, Black, Asian, and Hispanic Americans. *Policing & Society, 24,* 135–157.

Wu, Y., & Alteimer, I. (2013). Race/ethnicity, foreign-born status, and victimization in Seattle, WA. *Race and Justice: An International Journal, 3,* 339–357.

Wu, Y., Smith, B., & Sun, I. (2013). Race/ethnicity and perceptions of police bias: The case of Chinese immigrants. *Journal of Ethnicity in Criminal Justice, 11,* 71–92.

Wu, Y., Sun, I., & Smith, B. (2011). Race, immigration, and policing: Chinese immigrants' satisfaction with police. *Justice Quarterly, 28,* 745–774.

Wu, Y., Sun, I., & Triplett, R. (2009). Race, class or neighborhood context: Which matters more in measuring satisfaction with police? *Justice Quarterly, 26,* 125–156.

Wu, Y., & Wen, J. (2014). Fear of crime among Chinese immigrants in Metro-Detroit. *Crime, Law, and Social Change, 61,* 495–515.

Xie, Y., & Goyette, K. (2003). Social mobility and the educational choices of Asian Americans. *Social Science Research, 32,* 467–498.

Yakushko, O. (2009). Xenophobia: Understanding the roots and consequences of negative attitudes toward immigrants. *The Counseling Psychologist, 37,* 36–66.

Zhou, M., & Bankston, C. (1998). *Growing up American: How Vietnamese children adapt to life in the United States.* New York: Russell Sage.

Zmerli, S. (2012). Social structure and political trust in Europe: Mapping contextual preconditions of a relational concept. In S. Keil & O. Gabriel (Eds.), *Society and democracy in Europe* (pp. 111–138). New York: Routledge.

8

Summary and Conclusion

As a country built by immigrants, the U.S. has seen its immigration policies and their enforcement, particularly with respect to undocumented immigrants, in the center of its political debates in recent years. Since taking office in January 2017, President Trump has launched a series of highly restrictive Executive Orders and derivative measures that the likes of which have not been observed in decades. The recent **anti-immigration** activism and commitment to "build the wall" on the Mexican border signals the Trump administration's determination to move forward with a major overhaul of the country's immigration system. Such plans clearly have deep implications for police-community relations in general, and for immigrants' views of the police in their local communities in particular.

This book focuses on the nexus between race, ethnicity and immigration in the shaping of public attitudes toward the police among minority immigrant groups. Its focus is upon Hispanics, the Chinese, and Arabs—the three most major and rapidly growing immigrant groups in contemporary American society. The current administration's tough position and exclusionary measures on immigration policies, coupled with a greater involvement of local police forces in federal

© The Author(s) 2018
I. Y. Sun and Y. Wu, *Race, Immigration, and Social Control*,
Palgrave Studies in Race, Ethnicity, Indigeneity and Criminal Justice,
https://doi.org/10.1057/978-1-349-95807-8_8

immigration law enforcement, have given rise to great concern in much of the nation. An ongoing police "legitimacy crisis" triggered mainly by a series of deadly force incidents against African Americans has created a complex and fragile relationship between the police and numerous minority communities. Indeed, when foreign-born status intersects with race and ethnicity in the context of post 9/11 national security regime, minority immigrant groups and the police departments serving them have to overcome imposing barriers to the construction of positive relationships.

In the prior chapters we have emphasized the importance of race/ethnicity factors in the operation of U.S. policing. We have sought to explain how immigrant groups have been policed in the country over the years, and we have traced historical developments of policing Latino, Chinese and Arab immigrant communities. We have assembled empirical evidence associated with each group's evaluations of the police as well as comparison of groups, and proposed a conceptual framework for classifying the several theories that offer an account for immigrant perceptions of the police. This chapter synthesizes major findings from existing studies on the three immigrant groups' attitudes toward the police, pointing out directions for future research and suggesting policies and programs for bringing about better police-immigrant relations.

What We Have Learned

It is quite difficult, and requires much courage and risk-taking, to identify and summarize general patterns of attitudes and relationships that can apply to different immigrant groups in this country at the present time, knowing that the variations existing among and within these groups are considerable, yet the empirical data on them are in a severe shortage. Nonetheless, drawing upon the available evidence on public views of the police across the three main immigrant groups, we attempt to synthesize several tentative common cross-group findings in this concluding chapter. Our foremost observation is that past findings on the comparative ratings of the police by minority immigrants and non-immigrant, and non-Hispanic Whites are quite mixed, hence the conclusions derived by scholars tend to be rather equivocal. Studies employing either global indicators or more focused perceptual or attitudinal constructs to measure people's general judgments and specific sentiments towards the police show that immigrant minorities do not necessarily display more critical attitudes toward the police than do their non-Hispanic White counterparts. Unfortunately, reliable empirical evidence on the relative rankings of immigrants' evaluations of the police among Latinos, the Chinese and Arabs is completely lacking. However, it is nonetheless the case that the commonly-held belief of a non-Hispanic White–Asian–Hispanic–Black hierarchical ordering of regard for the police is clearly too simplistic a construct to account for immigrant groups' ratings of the police.

Second, the majority of immigrants regardless of their ethnic and racial background express favorable attitudes toward the police present in their community, a finding that is consistent with data from nationwide public opinion polls. Although immigrant groups are generally satisfied with the police and with the performance (competency and effectiveness) of police officers, there is some reliable evidence to suggest that immigrants tend to be more critical than their non-Hispanic White counterparts when offering assessments of police bias and fairness. As foreign-born individuals who may be subject to various types of anti-immigrant sentiments and social discrimination and who are unfamiliar with police procedures and practices in their host society, immigrants can be highly sensitive to unfair or biased policing, especially those who are not the most recent arrivals and have gained some knowledge about the power structure and relationship in the host country (Chu & Song, 2015; Skogan, 2005; Wu, Smith, & Sun, 2013). Likewise, aggressive counterterrorist measures geared toward certain ethnic groups tend to be seen as especially unfair and unduly stigmatizing (Sun, Wu, & Poteyeva, 2011). Worth mentioning, existing research on race and confidence in the police among the general public shows that when asked about specific police performance areas, especially those regarding unbiased policing, racial differences in responses tend to be larger than those in global/overall satisfaction responses (Cao & Wu, 2017). Similar patterns are also found among immigrant minorities in their perceptions of the police. Perhaps simply being racial/ethnic minorities serves to perpetuate minority immigrants' attitudes concerning the absence of full equality and justice under the law, a phenomenon commonly found among African Americans whose families' residence in the U.S. has spanned many generations (see Hagan & Albonetti, 1982; Henderson, Cullen, Cao, Browning, & Kopache, 1997; Rice & Piquero, 2005; Weitzer & Tuch, 2005).

Although it has been argued that the importance of racial status is diminishing in the lives of Americans in general (Wilson, 1987) and in accounting for public assessments of the police in particular (Jesilow, Meyer, & Namazzi, 1995), our own analysis of current evidence on the matter suggests strongly that race and ethnicity, intertwined with immigrant status, continue to largely define people's social attitudes toward legal authorities. More importantly, the interplay of race/ethnicity and immigration oftentimes seems to mitigate, rather than amplify, newcomers' potential negative assessments of the police. Neither race/ethnicity nor foreign-born status alone is sufficient to fully explain immigrants' attitudes toward the police. The conceptual framework that we proposed depicts the active interplay of a wide array of factors that should be considered when investigating perceptions of the police among Latino, Chinese, Arab, and other immigrant groups.

A final and related point to be made in this regard is that factors shaping immigrants' perceptions of the police in general are not so drastically different from those of the rest of American population. For example, similar to non-immigrants, immigrants' personal demographics are only weakly related to their assessments of the police. Meanwhile, some experiential, situational, contextual and immigrant-specific factors exert more significant effects on immigrants' perceptions of the police than demographic variables, with certain factors exercising a greater degree of impact on some immigrant groups than others. For example, immigrant-specific factors, such as language proficiency, country of origin, and immigration status appear to have a stronger correlation than individual demographics with Latinos' evaluations of the police. Experiential and contextual variables, such as police contact, media effects, and neighborhood conditions, are clearly associated with Chinese immigrants' assessments of the police. Some immigrant-specific variables, such as length of residence, perceptions of home country police, and evaluations of immigration officials, are linked to Chinese immigrants' perceptions of the U.S. police in certain ways. Confidence or trust in social institutions or groups, and perceived police procedural justice and effectiveness, shape Arab Americans' and immigrants' attitudes toward the police to a considerable extent. As not all existing studies on immigrant perceptions of the police utilize the same set of predictors, comparison of impact of covariates across groups remains challenging.

In brief, while minority immigrant groups are frequently subject to the negative connotations associated with the perpetuation of the "criminal aliens," "terrorist suspects," and "perpetual foreigners" social images actively spread by some elements of American society, such stereotyping does not automatically transfer into less favorable attitudes toward the police on the part of immigrants. Voluntary immigrants are inclined to come to this country with great hope and harbor admiration for the country. Nonetheless, it is clearly the case that their minority and/or immigrant status would seem to have a lingering effect on perceptions of whether fair and unbiased policing is taking place in their adopted homeland. Furthermore, immigrants' past and current experiences in both their home and host country, coupled with situational and contextual factors, are likely to make a difference in their perception of prevalence of fair and unbiased policing.

Directions for Future Research

Despite being large, rapidly growing immigrant groups in the U.S., immigrants with Latino, Chinese and Arab backgrounds have yet to receive the attention they deserve in the existing literature, with empirical research on their perceptions of the police and their experience with the justice system writ large remaining limited and consequently rather inconclusive in many respects. Differences in how samples have been drawn and what particular measurements have been employed in studies of minority and non-minority public opinions on the police make comparisons difficult. The need for substantially more research attention being given to these and other immigrant groups is unquestionable.

Accordingly, a few directions for future research are worth pointing out in this concluding chapter.

First, we strongly advocate empirical testing of the conceptual framework of immigrant perception of the police we proposed in the previous chapter. Understanding that a full test of all models or theories featured in the framework is extremely difficult, if not impossible, scholars could start their own inquiries by considering the applicability of different theories on immigrant groups with distinguishable group cultures and shared collective experiences. They could develop integrated models based on two or more of these theories which share common underlying assumptions. Theory competition and falsification meanwhile is most welcome. Continued efforts along this broad vein of inquiry are likely to yield evidence on the relative effects of these different explanations. Further, a developmental perspective on immigrant minorities' experience with and perceptions of the police in the U.S. should be considered. Factors influencing people's experience and perceptions are likely to change over time, and accordingly different theories may be particularly relevant to distinctive stages of the life course.

Second, recent research has shown a consistent impact of procedural justice on people's perceptions of the police (Tyler, 1990; Tyler & Huo, 2002; Wu et al., 2013). As unbiased and fair policing appears to be the performance area that divides ethnic minority and majority's confidence in the police the most, and immigrants are particularly sensitive to biased and unfair policing, it should be the area that garners most reform efforts. Performing procedural justice, accordingly, can be the arena most important and efficient for the police to work on to narrow group confidence gaps. Despite its popularity in the literature on the general public's assessments of the police, the process-based model of policing has yet to be adequately tested using immigrant populations. Further, even less is known regarding factors that affect police officers' willingness to provide procedural justice on the streets, including when interacting with immigrant groups. Recent studies have linked internal procedural justice that officers experience within police organizations to external procedural justice that officers render to citizens on the street (Van Craen, 2016; Wu, Sun, Chang, & Hsu, 2017). To have a more complete understanding of the antecedents of immigrants' views of the police, future research should also investigate the effect of internal/organizational procedural justice on external procedural justice, and subsequently on immigrants' evaluations of the police.

Third, more studies should be conducted to test the impact of contextual characteristics, including neighborhood-, city-, and even nation-level factors, on immigrants' perceptions of their host country police. Research that incorporates multilevel influences into analysis remains scarce, despite the fact that prior studies, albeit small in number, have consistently shown that community-level variables play an equally important, if not greater, role in determining public attitudes toward the police (Dunham & Alpert, 1988; Reisig & Parks, 2003; Sampson & Jeglum-Bartusch, 1998; Wu, Sun, & Triplett, 2009). Researchers should continue to elaborate and employ aggregate-level indicators, such as concentrated disadvantage, collective efficacy, racial composition, immigrant concentration, residential mobility and crime rate, in assessing immigrants' attitudes toward the police. More research attention should also be paid to the relationships present among these predictors. For example, does concentrated disadvantage lead to higher rates of violent crime which, in turn, result in less favorable evaluations of the police? Or, does extent of immigrant concentration lead to a changed level of collective efficacy, which further affects the relationship between formal social control agencies including the police and the immigrants they serve? To answer these questions, longitudinal data that follow neighborhoods over time can be most helpful in revealing causal relationships between aggregated level neighborhood factors and residents' perceptions of the local police. Further, going beyond neighborhood context, future research should explore the influence of subcultural values and norms in shaping immigrants' perceptions of the police. Such subculture can be connected to particular groups that are present both in the host and home community and country of immigrants.

Fourth, another important methodological consideration would be to explore immigrants' experience and perceptions in a broader range of locations. Understandably, previous research on Latino, Chinese and Arab immigrants has tended to rely on data from ethnic-majority or ethnic-concentrated communities and the cities in which they reside. These areas are a great starting point for research as they provide a large, relatively easy-to-access research population that also allows for systematic probability sampling. Such an approach, however, overlooks the emerging immigrant communities in many traditionally non-Latino, non-Asian or non-Arab cities or areas featuring a rapidly growing minority population. In the long term, the local populations studied should be expanded to immigrant populations in areas of different demographic profiles, non-metropolitan areas included, to verify the findings of the existing studies. For example, Arab Americans in non-Detroit areas may experience greater levels of backlash and more hate crimes than does the major ethnic-destination area of metro-Detroit. Such communities may also lack the social capital and political connections, and the various social and cultural organizations and civic associations whose support is often needed to garner reliable police protection.

Fifth, researchers should continue to compare and contrast immigrants with non-immigrants, particularly with respect to greater diversity in types of immigrant groups studied. Such research is needed to broaden our perspective regarding the patterns and correlates of people's experience with and perceptions of the police. To achieve this end, both quantitative and qualitative (e.g., ethnographic work) research is valuable; both forms of insight can complement one another in unpacking the sequence of events that link ethnicity, nationality and experience to perceptions, and identifying the relationship between group dynamics, ethnic culture, and the development of group-specific shared perceptions. Special attention should be paid to exploring measures that are capable of capturing the intricacies of group characteristics, ranging across the multiple dimensions of history, demography, structure, and culture.

Finally, researchers ought to watch closely and investigate in a timely way the impact of the Trump administration's restrictive immigration policies and orders on immigrant groups' perceptions of the police. An increasing involvement of local police in enforcing immigration laws and regulations creates a new source of potential conflict between immigrant communities and American law enforcement agencies, possibly reducing immigrants' trust in and satisfaction with the police over time. Similarly, recent strict and aggressive enforcement of new orders by immigration authorities may also cause a spill over negative effect on immigrants' evaluations of the police (Wu, Sun, & Smith, 2011).

The extent to which the war on illegal (and potentially legal as well) immigration may affect immigrants' perceptions of the police should be assessed and documented scientifically.

Policies and Programs to Consider

Policy makers and police administrators need to keep in mind that public trust of and confidence in the police is highly fragile, it is quite difficult to build, yet easy to destroy. Local and federal authorities should work diligently to establish healthy police-community relations, and to maintain strong social cohesion and stability within the communities they protect and serve. To start with, local law enforcement agencies should continue to recruit suitable, qualified individuals from within the immigrant communities in their communities into their ranks. Although police departments around the country have recognized the importance of having adequate representation from all social groups, attracting qualified immigrant women and men to the police work remains quite challenging, particularly for those who came from countries characterized by heavy reliance upon an authoritarian and abusive style of policing. A friendly working environment that does not discriminate against people from different backgrounds provides officers with fair opportunities for personal growth and career development. For most immigrant groups police employment offers reasonable compensation to employees and an honorable form of employment adding to the immigrant group's social status.

Local police agencies should be active participants in building social capital in immigrant communities. Many community-building policies and programs initiated by police departments under the broad theme of *community policing* have been introduced around the country. Such police efforts nonetheless have been less successful in communities where mutual trust between the police and local residents is low. While fair and quality policing remains influential in shaping people's views of police trustworthiness, keeping a long-term positive relationship with immigrant community organizations and news media deserves to be a routine task for the nation's police. Indeed, if the police are able to work regularly with existing community-based organizations to promote community networks in the service of efficacy and in the provision of public safety, the whole society will be better off. The police are capable of increasing local residents' mutual trust and cohesion, to reduce social disorganization and disorder, and to attract external capital building institutions; they can be active co-producers for the construction of strong immigrant communities, elements of American society which benefit not only local law enforcement but also the entire U.S. society.

Contrary to the potential benefits of being an active community builder, the police ought to be aware of the detrimental impact of overly aggressive enforcement on local communities, especially when vulnerable social groups are targeted. Aggressive strategies and tactics, whether stemming from traditional law-and-order policing thinking, political rhetoric, or crime control concerns, can potentially severely damage police-immigrant relations, disrupt social capital formation, and threaten family stability. Unfairly applied aggressive practices, especially, can seriously weaken police legitimacy and shaken the value foundation of this country with respect to social equity and rule of law. Instead, police departments should continue to reach out actively to immigrant communities, to explain the content of their field practices, and to debunk any myths associated with enforcement actions, as well as to reaffirm their commitment to due process and equal protection of the law.

Under the Trump administration, sanctuary cities, counties and states working to protect undocumented immigrants brave the risk of losing federal grants if they are unwilling to implement federal immigration policies, however draconian on their face. Similarly, incentives to engage actively in immigration enforcement by local police agencies is mounting because of new federal incentives and expanded police powers in the service of monitoring and controlling local immigrant populations. Local police departments need to be cautious about enforcing federal immigration laws, as by doing so, they may risk losing whatever hard-won trust and cooperation of immigrant communities they have earned. In many cases, trust that has been developed during the past few decades would be lost all too quickly.

Policy makers must understand the limitation of relying upon law enforcement agencies alone for gaining support from immigrant communities. Collective efforts to enhance the legitimacy of the entire government and gain reasonable respect from the citizens are plausible ways to maintain immigrants' positive attitudes toward the police. There is ample evidence indicating strong correlations between people's trust in different governmental agencies and political and legal institutions, and also preliminary evidence suggesting a close connection between immigrants' perceptions of immigration authorities and local police, illustrating one benefit of having sound immigration policies. Although it is not within the power of local police departments to regulate immigration officials' job performance and services, police agencies can take some measures to avoid the negative spillover effects of exclusivistic immigration policies and practices on themselves. For instance, special seminars can be organized for immigrants, introducing to them the functions of the U.S. police in crime control and service provision. They can inform immigrants about the differences and similarities between the roles of police officers and immigration officers, and advise them of the local police department's policy on enforcing or assisting in enforcing federal immigration laws. As immigrants may be more open to new information that their host country offers during early years of their migration, their views then can be more malleable or amenable if approached in this outreach way. Therefore, if police departments seek out and approach new immigrants in an educative and community-interactive context, they may be able to build positive police images both early on and continuously, leading to enhanced police legitimacy and mutually-trusting relations with immigrant communities.

References

Cao, L., & Wu, Y. (2017). Confidence in the police by race: Taking stock and charting new directions. *Police Practice and Research*. Accessed December 13, 2017 at http://www.tandfonline.com/doi/pdf/10.1080/15614263.2017.1396460?needAccess=true.

Chu, D., & Song, J. (2015). A comparison of Chinese immigrants' perceptions of the police in New York City and Toronto. *Crime & Delinquency, 61*, 402–427.

Dunham, R., & Alpert, G. (1988). Neighborhood differences in attitudes toward policing: Evidence for a mixed-strategy model of policing in a multi-ethnic setting. *Journal of Criminal Law & Criminology, 79,* 504–523.

Hagan, J., & Albonetti, C. (1982). Race, class and the perception of criminal injustice in America. *American Journal of Sociology, 88,* 329–355.

Henderson, M., Cullen, F., Cao, L., Browning, S., & Kopache, R. (1997). The impact of race on perceptions of criminal injustice. *Journal of Criminal Justice, 25,* 447–462.

Jesilow, P., Meyer, J., & Namazzi, N. (1995). Public attitudes toward the police. *American Journal of the Police, 14,* 67–88.

Reisig, M., & Parks, R. (2003). Neighborhood context, police behavior, and satisfaction with police. *Justice Research and Policy, 3,* 37–65.

Rice, S., & Piquero, A. (2005). Perceptions of discrimination and justice in New York City. *Policing: An International Journal of Police Strategies & Management, 28,* 98–117.

Sampson, R., & Jeglum-Bartusch, D. (1998). Legal cynicism and (subcultural?) tolerance of deviance: The neighborhood context of racial differences. *Law and Society Review, 32,* 777–804.

Skogan, W. (2005). Citizen satisfaction with police encounters. *Police Quarterly, 8,* 298–321.

Sun, I., Wu, Y., & Poteyeva, M. (2011). Arab Americans' support for counter-terrorism measures: The impact of race, ethnicity, and religion. *Studies in Conflict and Terrorism, 34,* 540–555.

Tyler, T. (1990). *Why people obey the law.* New Haven, CT: Yale University Press.

Tyler, T., & Huo, Y. (2002). *Trust in the law. Encouraging public cooperation with the police and courts.* New York: Russell Sage.

Van Craen, M. (2016). Understanding police officers' trust and trustworthy behavior: A work relations framework. *European Journal of Criminology, 13,* 274–294.

Weitzer, R., & Tuch, S. (2005). Determinants of public satisfaction with the police. *Police Quarterly, 8,* 279–297.

Wilson, W. (1987). *The declining significance of race.* Chicago: University of Chicago Press.

Wu, Y., Smith, B., & Sun, I. (2013). Race/ethnicity and perceptions of police bias: The case of Chinese immigrants. *Journal of Ethnicity in Criminal Justice, 11,* 71–92.

Wu, Y., Sun, I., Chang, C., & Hsu, K. (2017). Procedural justice received and given: Supervisory treatment, emotional states and behavioral compliance among Taiwanese police officers. *Criminal Justice and Behavior, 44,* 963–982.

Wu, Y., Sun, I., & Smith, B. (2011). Race, immigration and policing: Chinese immigrants' satisfaction with police. *Justice Quarterly, 28,* 745–777.

Wu, Y., Sun, I., & Triplett, R. (2009). Race, class or neighborhood context: Which matters more in measuring satisfaction with police? *Justice Quarterly, 26,* 125–156.

Index

© The Editor(s) (if applicable) and The Author(s) 2018
I. Y. Sun and Y. Wu, *Race, Immigration, and Social Control*,
Palgrave Studies in Race, Ethnicity, Indigeneity and Criminal Justice,
https://doi.org/10.1057/978-1-349-95807-8

Printed in the United States
By Bookmasters